AIR FRYER COOKBOOK

Amazingly Easy Recipes to Fry, Bake, Grill, and Roast with Your Air Fryer

Brenda Sullivan

© Copyright 2020 by Brenda Sullivan- All rights reserved.

The content contained within this book may not be reproduced, duplicated, or transmitted without direct written permission from the author or the publisher.

Under no circumstances will any blame or legal responsibility be held against the publisher, or author, for any damages, reparation, or monetary loss due to the information contained within this book. Either directly or indirectly. You are responsible for your own choices, actions, and results.

Legal Notice:

This book is copyright protected. This book is only for personal use. You cannot amend, distribute, sell, use, quote or paraphrase any part, or the content within this book, without the consent of the author or publisher.

Disclaimer Notice:

Please note the information contained within this document is for educational and entertainment purposes only. All effort has been executed to present accurate, up to date, and reliable, complete information. No warranties of any kind are declared or implied.

Readers acknowledge that the author is not engaging in the endearing of legal, financial, medical, or professional advice. The content within this book has been derived from various sources.

Please consult a licensed professional before attempting any techniques outlined in this book.

By reading this document, the reader agrees that under no circumstances is the author responsible for any losses, direct or indirect, which are incurred as a result of the use of the information contained within this document, including, but not limited to, — errors, omissions, or inaccuracies.

Table of Contents

What is An Air Fryer?...**10**
- How to Use Your Air Fryer
- The Benefits of Air fryer
- Measurement Conversion Table

Breakfast Recipes...**15**
- Air Fried Eggs
- French Toast Stuffed with Blueberry Cream Cheese
- Feta Triangles
- Pizza Rolls
- BBQ Chicken Salad with Onion Straws
- Roasted Garlic and Thyme Dipping Sauce
- Scotch Eggs
- Crispy Falafel
- Tahini Sauce
- Avocado Egg Rolls
- Cilantro Honey

Lunch Recipes..**34**
- Portabella Pepperoni Pizza
- Personal Pizzas
- Chicken Nuggets
- Chicken Fajitas
- Honey Glazed Chicken Wings

- Bacon Wrapped Shrimp
- Southern Air Fried Catfish
- Buffalo Cauliflower Steaks

Dinner Recipes..**51**

- Roasted Rack of Lamb with Macadamia Crust
- Barbeque Chicken
- Mediterranean Chicken Wings with Olives
- Chicken Buffalo Drummies
- Cornish Hen
- Basic Air Fried Chicken
- Black Bean Burger
- General Tso's Chicken

Poultry Recipes..**66**

- Country Chicken Tenders
- Buffalo Chicken Tenders
- Korean BBQ Satay
- Jerk Chicken Wings
- Fried Chicken Tenders with Mustard and Sage
- Parmesan Crusted Chicken Fillet
- Crispy and Sweet Chicken Wings
- Chicken Parmesan

Pork Recipes..**82**

- Pizza Rolls

- Pigs in a Blanket
- Bacon Wrapped Dates with Blue Cheese
- Asian Style Baby Back Ribs
- Tortilla Crusted Pork Loin Chops
- Cheddar Bacon Croquettes
- Jalapeno Bacon Poppers
- Jamaican Jerk Pork

Beef Recipes..**95**

- Fried Meatballs in Tomato Sauce
- Mini Cheeseburger
- Sliders Chimichurri
- Skirt Steak
- Stuffed Peppers
- Steak with Garlic Herb Butter Meatloaf

Seafood Recipes **106**

- Crab Croquettes
- Cod Fish Nuggets
- Fish Tacos
- Fish with Chips
- Tuna Melt Sandwich
- Salmon with Dill Sauce
- Cajun Shrimp
- Banging Shrimp

- Coconut Shrimp
- Teriyaki Glazed Halibut Steak
- Cajun Style Fried Shrimp
- Cod Fingers
- Sesame Encrusted Ahi Tuna with Hoisin Sauce
- Crab Cakes

Vegetable Recipes..131

- Stuffed Garlic Mushrooms
- Mushroom, Onion and Feta Frittata
- Asparagus Frittata
- Fried Green Tomatoes
- Crusty Potato Wedges
- Noodley Kebabs
- Vegetable Croquettes
- Marinated Artichoke Hearts

Side Dishes..145

- Fried Avocado Tacos
- Roasted Heirloom Tomato with Baked Feta Cheese Sticks
- Sweet Potato Fries Air Fried Potato Skins
- Tuscan Style Potato Wedges Crispy Brussels Sprouts

Appetizer..**159**
- Grilled Cheese
- Fried Mac and Cheese Balls
- Easy Baked Mac and Cheese
- Crispy Potato Skin Wedges
- Potato Croquettes
- Crunchy Eggplant Fries
- Smoked Paprika and Parmesan Potato Wedges
- Zucchini Wedges

Snacks..**173**
- Barbeque Corn Sandwich
- Grilled Scallion Cheese Sandwich Corn Bread
- Corn Rolls French Fries Snack Mix
- Potatoes Au Gratin
- Rosemary Russet Potato Chips Fair Fries
- Crunchy Onion Rings
- Yummy Donuts
- French Fries with Vegan Mushroom Gravy

Desserts..**188**
- Vanilla Soufflé
- Chocolate Marshmallow Bread Pudding
- Chocolate Cake Version 1
- Chocolate Cake Version 2

- Apricot Blackberry Crumble
- Peanut Butter Marshmallow Fluff Turnovers
- White Chocolate Raspberry Cheesecake Rolls
- Fried Dough
- Pumpkin Cupcakes
-

Conclusion 208

Preface

This book contains proven steps and strategies on how to start preparing healthy and delicious meals that you can serve any time of the day using only one appliance – the Air Fryer. This innovation makes it possible to enjoy fried foods with less oil. You can also use it to whip up a wide range of dishes, snacks, and desserts.

It features loads of recipes that you can tweak in many ways to suit your preference and the availability of ingredients. Each recipe has a nutrient content guide per serving. In addition, it explains the basics about the appliance and the benefits of using it as compared to the traditional manner of frying food.

Finally, it also contains a quick guide of measurement conversion that can become handy when preparing your ingredients. Without further ado, lets get started!

What is An Air Fryer?

An air fryer utilizes the convection mechanism in cooking food. It circulates hot air through the use of a mechanical fan to cook the ingredients inside the fryer. The process eliminates the use of too much oil in the traditional way of frying but still cooks food via the Maillard effect (i.e. a chemical reaction between an amino acid and a reducing sugar, usually requiring the addition of heat).

The process was named after the person who first explained it in 1912, French chemist Louis-Camille Maillard. The effect gives a distinctive flavor to browned foods, such as bread, biscuits, cookies, pan-fried meat, seared steaks, and many more.

The air fryer requires only a thin layer of oil for the ingredients to cook. It circulates hot air up to 392 degrees Fahrenheit. It's an innovative way of eliminating up to 80 percent of the oil that is traditionally used to fry different foods and prepare pastries.

You can find a dose of friendly features in air fryers depending on the brand you're using. Most brands include a timer adjustment and temperature control setting to make cooking easier and precise. An air fryer comes with a cooking basket where you'll place the food. The basket is placed on top of a drip tray. Depending on the model you're using, you will either be prompted to shake the basket to distribute oil evenly or it automatically does the job via a food agitator.

This is perfect for home use but if you're cooking for many people and you want to apply the same cooking technique, you can put your food items in specialized air crisper trays and cook them using a convection oven. An air fryer and convection oven apply the same technique in cooking but an air fryer has a smaller built and produces less heat.

How to Use Your Air Fryer

This appliance comes with a manual for easy assembly and as a handy guide for first-time users. Most brands also include a pamphlet of recipes to give you ideas about the wide range of dishes that you can create using this single kitchen appliance. Once you are ready to cook and you have all your ingredients ready, put them in the basket and insert it into the fryer. Other recipes will require you to preheat the air fryer before using. Once the basket is in, set the temperature and timer and begin cooking.

You can use an air fryer to cook food in a variety of ways. Once you get used with the basics, you can try its other features, such as advanced baking and using air fryer dehydrators.

Here are some of the cooking techniques that you can do with this single appliance:

Fry: You can actually omit oil in cooking but a little amount adds crunch and flavor to your food. You can add oil to the ingredients while mixing or lightly spray the food with oil before cooking. You can use most kinds of oils but many users prefer peanut, olive, sunflower, and canola oils.

Roast: You can produce the same quality of roasted foods like the ones cooked in a conventional roaster in a faster manner.

This is recommended to people who need to come up with a special dish but do not have much time to prepare.

Bake: There are baking pans suited for this appliance that you can use to bake bread, cookies, and other pastries. It only takes around 15 to 30 minutes to get your baked goodies done.

Grill: It effectively grills your food easily and without mess. You only need to shake the basket halfway through the cooking process or flip the ingredients once or twice depending on the instructions. To make it easier, you can put the ingredients in a grill pan or grill layer with a handle, which other models include in the package or you can also buy one as an added accessory.

There are many kinds of foods that you can cook using an air fryer, but there are also certain types that are not suited for it. Avoid cooking ingredients, which can be steamed, like beans and carrots. You also cannot fry foods covered in heavy batter in this appliance.

Aside from the above mentioned, you can cook most kinds of ingredients using an air fryer. You can use it to cook foods covered in light flour or bread crumbs.

You can cook a variety of vegetables in the appliance, such as cauliflower, asparagus, zucchini, kale, peppers, and corn on the cob. You can also use it to cook frozen foods and home prepared meals by following a different set of instructions for these purposes.

An air fryer also comes with another useful feature - the separator. It allows you to cook multiple dishes at a time. Use the separator to divide ingredients in the pan or basket. You have to make sure that all ingredients have the same temperature setting so that everything will cook evenly at the same time.

The Benefits of Airfryer

It is important to note that air fried foods are still fried. Unless you've decided to eliminate the use of oils in cooking, you must still be cautious about the food you eat. Despite that, it clearly presents a better and healthier option than deep-frying. It helps you avoid unnecessary fats and oils, which makes it an ideal companion when you intend to lose weight. It offers a lot more benefits, which include the following:

It is convenient and easy to use, plus, it's easy to clean. It doesn't give off unwanted smells when cooking.

You can use it to prepare a variety of meals. It can withstand heavy cooking.

It is durable and made of metal and high-grade plastic.

Cooking using this appliance is not as messy as frying in a traditional way. You don't have to worry about greasy spills and stains in the kitchen.

Measurement Conversion Table

Measurement	Conversion
1 stick of butter	1/2 cup or 8 tablespoons
4 quarts	1 gallon
2 quarts	1/2 gallon
1 cup	8 fluid ounces or 1/2 pint or 16 tablespoons
2 cups	1 pint
1 quart	32 ounces or 2 pints or 4 cups
4 tablespoons	1/4 cup
8 tablespoons	1/2 cup

1/2 tablespoon   1 1/2 teaspoons
3 teaspoons   1 tablespoon

Breakfast Recipes

Air Fried Eggs

Nutritional Facts/Calories: 256 calories, 20.6g fat, 1.4g carbohydrates, 16.5g protein

Preparation + Cook Time: 30 minutes

Servings: 4

Ingredients:

1 tablespoon extra-virgin olive oil Salt and pepper to taste

4 bacon slices

4 eggs

2 cups baby spinach (rinsed and drained) 1/2 cup shredded cheddar cheese (divided)

Instructions:

1. Heat oil in a pan over medium-high flame. Put the spinach and cook until wilted. Transfer to a plate and drain excess liquid. Transfer them into 4 greased ramekins.

2. Add a slice of bacon and egg to each ramekin. Sprinkle cheese on top. Season with salt and pepper.

3. Arrange the ramekins inside the cooking basket of the Air Fryer. Cook for 15 minutes at 350 degrees.

French Toast Stuffed with Blueberry Cream Cheese

Nutritional Facts/Calories: 182 calories, 4.1g fat, 27g carbohydrates, 9.9g protein

Preparation + Cook Time: 18 minutes

Servings: 4

Ingredients:

4 tablespoons whipped cream cheese (berry-flavored) 2 eggs (beaten)

4 2-inch slices of Challah bread 3 teaspoons sugar

1/3 cup whole milk

1/4 cup fresh blueberries 1/4 teaspoon salt

1/4 teaspoon ground nutmeg

1 1/2 cups crumbled corn flakes

Directions/Instructions:

1. In a bowl, mix to combine the eggs, salt, sugar, nutmeg, and milk.

2. Put the whipped cream cheese in another bowl and fold in the blueberries.

3. Slit the top part of each Challah bread. Add 2 tablespoons of the berry mixture to each slice. Soak the stuffed bread slices in the egg mixture until completely coated. Cover them with corn flakes and gently press to make them stick.

4. Arrange the stuffed bread slices in the cooking basket of the Air Fryer. Cook for 8 minutes at 400 degrees.

Note: This is best served while warm. You can opt to drizzle it with maple syrup or add a bit of butter.

Feta Triangles

Nutritional Facts/Calories: 144 calories, 11.8g fat, 5.8g carbohydrates, 4.5g protein

Preparation + Cook Time: 25 minutes
Servings: 5

Ingredients:
2 sheets of frozen filo pastry (thawed)
2 tablespoons flat-leafed parsley (minced) Ground black pepper
2 tablespoons olive oil 4 ounces feta cheese 1 scallion (minced)
1 egg yolk

Directions/Instructions:

1. Whisk the egg yolk, scallion, parsley, and feta in a bowl until combined. Season with pepper.

2. Cut each filo sheet into 3 strips. Place a teaspoon of the feta mixture in each strip. Fold the sheet and roll all the filling is covered.

3. Lightly brush each filo with oil. Arrange 6 feta triangles in the cooking basket at a time. Cook for 3 minutes at 390 degrees. Cook for 2 more minutes at 360 degrees.

Pizza Rolls

Nutritional Facts/Calories: 420 calories, 11.8g fat, 61.1g carbohydrates, 16.2g protein

Preparation + Cook Time: 50 minutes

Servings: 6

Ingredients:

1 4-ounce jar of pizza sauce

2 pieces Italian sausage (cooked and crumbled) 1 onion (chopped)

15 egg roll wrappers

2 cups whole milk mozzarella (shredded) 2 red peppers (roasted and chopped)

3 ounces sliced pepperoni (chopped) 1 teaspoon garlic powder

Directions/Instructions:

1. Mix the peppers, cheese, onions, pepperoni, and sausage in a bowl. Keep on mixing as you add the garlic powder and pizza sauce.

2. Scoop 1/4 of the mixture into each egg roll wrapper. Fold all sides until the filling is wrapped. Moisten the last fold to secure. Roll it tightly. Perform the same steps with the rest of the wrappers. Put in a covered container and freeze overnight.

3. Put 5 pieces of the pizza rolls in the cooking basket at a time. Make sure that you do not overcrowd the pan because they will expand quite a lot. Lightly spray them with a non-stick cooking spray.

4. Cook for 7 minutes at 400 degrees. Flip them and continue cooking for 2 more minutes. Transfer to a platter and repeat the process with the rest of the rolls.

5. Serve the rolls with pizza sauce for dipping.

Note: You can also serve them with cheese or yogurt.

BBQ Chicken Salad with Onion Straws

Nutritional Facts/Calories: 683 calories, 19.7g fat, 74.3g carbohydrates, 57.4g protein

Preparation + Cook Time: 35 minutes

Servings: 4

Ingredients:
3 green onions (chopped) 12 grape tomatoes (sliced)
1 cup Monterey Jack cheese (shredded) 1 can French fried onions
1 pound chicken tenders (boneless) 3 tablespoons BBQ sauce
2 ears of corn (hulled)

1 tablespoon brown sugar

3 tablespoons chopped fresh cilantro leaves

1 cup canned black beans (drained and rinsed) 1 teaspoon paprika

1 teaspoon sea salt 1/4 cup ranch dressing

1/2 head of romaine lettuce (rinsed, patted dry and sliced into strips)

1/2 head of iceberg lettuce (rinsed, patted dry and sliced into strips)

1/2 teaspoon garlic powder 1/2 teaspoon pepper

Directions/Instructions:

1. Lightly spray each ear of corn with some oil and then place them in the cooking basket. Cook for 10 minutes at 400 degrees.

2. Mix to combine brown sugar, pepper, garlic powder, paprika, and salt in a bowl. Place the meat in the mixture and toss to coat.

3. Transfer the cooked corn to a platter and leave to cool. Cut the kernels off the cob and place them in a bowl.

4. Arrange the coated chicken tenders in the cooking basket and lightly spray with oil. Cook for 10 minutes at 400 degrees. Flip the meat halfway through the process. Transfer the cooked meat to a chopping board and dice.

5. Toss the diced meat, corn kernels and the rest of the ingredients, except for the French fried onions. Toss until combined.

6. Top with the onions before serving.

Note: You can replace chicken tenders with other meat, such as turkey, beef, or lamb. Adjust the cooking time until the meat is done.

Roasted Garlic and Thyme Dipping Sauce

Nutritional Facts/Calories: 485 calories, 39.4g fat, 34.1g carbohydrates, 2.2g protein

Preparation + Cook Time: 35 minutes

Servings: 1

Ingredients:

1/8 teaspoon pepper 1/8 teaspoon salt

1/2 teaspoon fresh thyme leaves (minced) 2 tablespoons roasted garlic (crushed) 1/2 cup light mayonnaise

Directions/Instructions:

1. Wrap garlic in foil. Put it in the cooking basket of the Air Fryer and roast for 30 minutes at 390 degrees.

2. You can make this sauce ahead of time and refrigerate until ready to serve. Simply mix all ingredients until combined.

Note: You can serve this sauce along with a variety of dishes and snacks.

Scotch Eggs

Nutritional Facts/Calories: 308 calories, 24.4g fat, 0.6g carbohydrates, 20.6g protein

Preparation + Cook Time: 25 minutes

Servings: 6

Ingredients:1/4 cup grated Parmesan cheese

3/4 pound sausage (you can use homemade) 6 large eggs

Directions/Instructions:

1. Fill a pot with water and bring to a boil. Put the eggs, reduce the heat to low, and cook for 7 minutes. Transfer the eggs in a bowl and immediately rinse with cold water. Peel them and set aside.

2. Place the sausage on a chopping board and divide into 6. Put each piece in between two pieces of wax paper or plastic wrap. Roll it according to your desired size. Peel off the top sheet and add the egg and wrap it inside the flattened sausage. Peel off the remaining sheet of wax paper. Perform the same step to the remaining sausages and eggs.

3. Roll each piece in grated Parmesan cheese.

4. Preheat the Air Fryer to 400 degrees.

5. Arrange the Scotch eggs in the cooking basket and lightly spray them with oil. Cook for 14 minutes.

Note: You can eat this warm or cold. If you want them to be a bit crunchy, use panko breadcrumbs instead of Parmesan cheese as a coating. Try different sauces or dipping with the dish. If you will be using a convection oven instead, set the temperature to 400 degrees.

Crispy Falafel

Nutritional Facts/Calories: 103 calories, 1.7g fat 17.4g carbohydrates, 5.4g protein

Preparation + Cook Time: 35 minutes

Servings: 30 balls

Ingredients:

2 garlic cloves (minced) 1 onion (finely chopped)

2 cups dried chickpeas (soaked overnight) 1 1/2 teaspoons sea salt

1/2 teaspoon cayenne pepper

1 teaspoon ground black pepper 2 teaspoons ground coriander

2 teaspoons cumin powder 1 tablespoon chickpea flour

1/4 cup cilantro leaves (chopped)

3/4 cup flat-leaf parsley leaves (chopped)

Directions/Instructions:

1. Put all ingredients in a food processor and process until minced and combined. Make sure that you don't overmix. Transfer the mixture to a bowl.

2. Use your hands to shape the mixture into 30 pieces of small balls.

3. Arrange 9 balls in the cooking basket at a time and lightly spray them with oil. Cook for 15 minutes at 380 degrees. Transfer to a platter and cook the rest of the falafel balls.

Note: You can prepare the falafel balls ahead of time. Put them on a cookie sheet and freeze for an hour. Transfer them to a covered container and freeze until ready to use. Serve them with your preferred sauce or dipping. You can also try eating them along with tahini sauce.

Tahini Sauce

Ingredients:

Sea salt to taste

2 tablespoons water (adjust according to preference) 1/2 garlic clove (minced)

1/2 lemon (juiced)

2 teaspoons maple syrup 1/4 cup tahini

Directions/Instructions:

1. Put the tahini, salt, garlic paste, lemon juice, and maple syrup in a small bowl. Mix until combined. Add a tablespoon of water at a time. Mix well. Add more water until you have achieved your preferred consistency.

Avocado Egg Rolls

Nutritional Facts/Calories: 531 calories, 31.8g fat, 55.2g carbohydrates, 11.4g protein

Preparation + Cook Time: 20 minutes

Servings: 4

Ingredients:

1 large egg (beaten) Salt and pepper to taste 8 egg roll wrappers

2 tablespoons fresh lime juice 1 garlic clove (minced)

3 vocados (halved, pitted, and diced) 1 Roma tomato

1/4 cup red onion

2 tablespoons chopped cilantro

Directions/Instructions:

1. Put garlic, lime juice, cilantro, onion, tomato, and avocado in a bowl. Gently mix until combined. Season with salt and pepper.

2. Moisten the edges of the wrapper with the beaten egg. Scoop 1/3 cup of the avocado filling in each wrapper. Roll the wrapper to cover the filling and seal the edge. Repeat the step with the remaining wrappers and filling.

3. Preheat the Air Fryer to 400 degrees.

4. Lightly spray the cooking basket with oil. Brush the egg rolls with the remaining egg wash and arrange them in the cooking basket. Cook for 5 minutes, flip them and continue cooking for 5 more minutes.

5. Transfer to a platter and serve once cooled.

Note: You can serve the dish along with different kinds of sauces and dipping. You can also try eating them along with Cilantro Honey Dipping Sauce.

Lunch Recipes

Portabella Pepperoni Pizza

Nutritional Facts/Calories: 320 calories, 28.8g fat, 3.3g carbohydrates, 13.9g protein

Preparation + Cook Time: 11 minutes

Servings: 3

Ingredients:

12 pepperoni slices

3 tablespoons shredded mozzarella cheese 3 tablespoons tomato sauce

3 tablespoons olive oil

3 portabella mushroom caps (rinsed and scooped) A pinch of dried Italian seasonings

A pinch of salt

Directions/Instructions:

1. Pour a bit of oil on both sides of the mushroom caps. Season the inner part with Italian seasonings and salt. Drizzle tomato sauce on top and add cheese. Arrange them in the cooking basket. Cook for 1 minute at 330 degrees.

2. Add pepperoni slices on top of each portabella and continue cooking for 5 more minutes.

3. Transfer to a plate and serve while warm.

Note: You can sprinkle more cheese while the dish is still hot. You can also opt to sprinkle them with crushed red pepper flakes.

Personal Pizzas

Nutritional Facts/Calories: 207 calories, 10.4g fat, 23.1g carbohydrates, 6.7g protein

Preparation + Cook Time: 45 minutes

Servings: 2

Ingredients:

1/2 cup of mozzarella cheese (shredded) 1/4 cup of Parmesan cheese (grated)

A pinch of garlic powder A pinch of dried oregano 1 can of pizza crust

1 tablespoon olive oil

1/2 cup pizza sauce (store-bought or homemade) Toppings of your choice

Directions/Instructions:

1. Cut the dough into 4 and roll each piece into a ball. Rub them with olive oil and stretch each dough ball in a pizza pan.

2. Spread 1/4 of the sauce to each stretched dough in the pan. Add 1 tablespoon of parmesan, 2 tablespoons of mozzarella cheese, a pinch of garlic powder and a pinch of dried oregano on top. Add your preferred toppings.

3. Place a rack in the cooking basket and put the pizza pan on top of it. Cook for 6 minutes at 350 degrees.

4. Transfer to a plate and slice into 4.

5. Repeat the steps to cook the remaining dough.

Note: Adjust the nutri info depending on the toppings used. You can try adding different toppings depending on your preference. You can use pepperoni, ham, mushrooms, pineapple, crumbled sausage, meatballs, peppers, and many more.

Chicken Nuggets

Nutritional Facts/Calories: 356 calories, 9.3g fat, 27.2g carbohydrates, 38.2g protein

Preparation + Cook Time: 45 minutes

Servings: 4

Ingredients:

1 cup buttermilk

1 teaspoon salt

1/2 teaspoon garlic powder 1/2 teaspoon paprika

1 pound chicken breasts (skinless and boneless, chopped) 1 cup flour

Directions/Instructions:

1. Place meat in a bowl and cover with buttermilk. Leave for an hour or overnight to marinate.

2. In a bowl, mix flour, garlic powder, paprika, and salt until well combined. Add the meat and toss until coated. Arrange 8 chicken nuggets in the cooking basket at a time. Lightly spray them with oil.

3. Cook for 10 minutes at 400 degrees.

4. Transfer to a platter and cook the remaining nuggets.

Note: Serve the dish with a variety of sauces for dipping.

Chicken Fajitas

Nutritional Facts/Calories: 426 calories, 20.1g fat, 21.5g carbohydrates, 40g protein

Preparation + Cook Time: 34 minutes

Servings: 4

Ingredients:

4 flour tortillas (premade) 1/2 teaspoon sea salt

1/2 teaspoon chili powder

1/4 teaspoon ground coriander 1/4 teaspoon ground cumin

1/4 teaspoon ground black pepper

1 pound chicken breasts (cut into strips) 1 onion (peeled and chopped)

1 green pepper (cored and sliced) 1 red pepper (cored and sliced)

1 tablespoon fresh lime juice 1 teaspoon garlic powder

For garnishing

1 cup lettuce (shredded) 1/2 cup medium salsa 1/2 cup sour cream

1/2 cup shredded cheddar cheese

Directions/Instructions:

1. In a bowl, put the coriander, garlic powder, salt, cumin, chili powder, and pepper. Mix well. Add the meat and lime juice. Stir and leave to marinate for 10 minutes. Add the peppers and onion, and toss to combine.

2. Put half of the mixture in the cooking basket of the Air Fryer. Spray it with non-stick cooking spray. Set the fryer to 400 degrees and cook for 8 minutes. Transfer to a platter and cook the remaining mixture.

3. Put the tortillas in the cooking basket. Set the fryer to 190 degrees and cook for 3 minutes.

4. Divide the cooked meat as filling for the tortillas. Serve with the ingredients for garnishing.

Honey Glazed Chicken Wings

Nutritional Facts/Calories: 193 calories, 11.1g fat, 10.8g carbohydrates, 11g protein

Preparation + Cook Time: 30 minutes

Servings: 4

Ingredients:

Honey

1 onion (thinly sliced)

7 medium-sized chicken wings

For the marinade

1/8 teaspoon pepper

1/2 teaspoon five-spice powder 1/2 teaspoon ginger (chopped) 1/2 teaspoon garlic (chopped) 1/4 teaspoon sugar

1 tablespoon Chinese cooking wine 1/2 tablespoon soy sauce

Directions/Instructions:

1. Rinse the meat and pat them dry.

2. Combine all ingredients for the marinade in a bowl. Add the meat and leave to marinate for an hour or overnight.

3. Spread the onion slices on a pan. Lay the meat on top.

4. Put the rack inside the cooking basket and place the pan on top. Cook for 10 minutes at 350 degrees. Flip the meat and brush with honey. Cook for 5 more minutes. Flip and brush with honey. Cook for 5 more minutes.

Note: Honey makes the cooked meat appear glossy.

Bacon Wrapped Shrimp

Nutritional Facts/Calories: 1 calories, 4g fat, 0.2g carbohydrates, 3.7g protein, 12mg cholesterol, 222mg sodium

Preparation + Cook Time: 15 minutes

Servings: 12

Ingredients:

12 jumbo shrimp (peeled and deveined) 6 strips thinly sliced bacon (cut in half)

Directions/Instructions:

1. Place a slice of bacon on a cutting board and put the shrimp on top. Wrap the bacon from the tail end of the shrimp up to the other end. Repeat the step with the rest of the shrimp.

2. Arrange the bacon wrapped shrimp pieces in the cooking basket and lightly spray with oil.

3. Cook for 12 minutes in a preheated Air Fryer at 390 degrees.

Note: You can also cook this dish in a convection toaster oven set at 400 degrees.

Southern Air Fried Catfish

Nutritional Facts/Calories: 227 calories, 14.6g fat, 3g carbohydrates, 21.1g protein

Preparation + Cook Time: 15 minutes

Servings: 4

Ingredients:

1/2 cup almond meal

1 teaspoon lemon pepper 1 egg white (beaten)

1 pound fresh catfish fillets (sliced into 2-inch strips)

Directions/Instructions:

1. Beat the egg white in a bowl until foamy. Put the catfish strips and gently mix until coated.

2. Put the almond meal and lemon pepper in a Ziploc bag. Seal the bag and shake until combined. Add the fish strips and gently shake until coated.

3. Arrange the coated fish strips in the cooking basket. Cook for 12 minutes in a preheated Air Fryer at 390 degrees.

Note: To make the dish a classic Southern meal, you can add black eyed peas and tomato slices on top before serving.ù

Buffalo Cauliflower Steaks

Nutritional Facts/Calories: 304 calories, 3g fat, 60.4 carbohydrates, 10.1g protein

Preparation + Cook Time: 30 minutes

Servings: 4

Ingredients:

1 head of cauliflower (large) Salt and pepper to taste

1 cup buffalo sauce Dry ingredients

1 tablespoon paprika

1 tablespoon salt

1 tablespoon onion powder 1 tablespoon garlic powder

2 teaspoons cayenne (optional) 1/3 cup cornstarch

1 1/2 cups all-purpose flour Wet ingredients

1 tablespoon hot sauce 2 tablespoons bourbon

2 tablespoons egg powder (mixed with 1/2 cup ice cold water) 1 cup soy milk (mixed with 2 teaspoons apple cider vinegar)

Directions/Instructions:

1. Prepare the cauliflower. Place the cauliflower head on a cutting board and slice into 2. Cut each half into 2. Chop the remaining portion into florets.

2. Put water in a pot over high flame. Add salt and bring to a boil. Turn the heat to medium and add the cauliflower florets. Cook for a minute. Transfer to a cookie sheet, sprinkle with salt and place on top of a wire rack. Leave to cool.

3. Prepare the breading. Put all the dry ingredients in a bowl. Mix until combined. Put all the wet ingredients in another bowl and mix well.

4. Coat each piece of the steak and florets with the dry mixture. Tap off excess mixture before putting them back on a wire rack. Repeat the step until you're done with the rest of the steaks and florets.

5. Scoop 3 tablespoons of the wet mixture to the remaining dry mixture. Use a spatula to combine the mixture.

6. Dip each piece of the steak and florets into the wet mixture and coat each with the moistened flour. Use your hands to press and make the coating stick. Put them back on the wire rack. Refrigerate for 30 minutes.

7. Lightly spray the battered cauliflower steaks with oil. Arrange them in the cooking basket and cook for 10 minutes at 400 degrees. Flip the pieces halfway through the process.

8. Put the buffalo sauce in a bowl. Dip each cooked steak in the sauce until coated. Put all pieces in the cooking basket and cook each side for 4 minutes.

9. Repeat the same sequence in cooking the florets but adjust the time since they cook faster.

Note: You can use this as rice toppings or pair it with other dishes. You can also use it as filling to hamburger buns drizzled with your preferred dressing. If you want to make your own buffalo sauce, simply put the same amount of vinegar-based hot sauce and melted butter in a bowl and mix until combined.

Dinner Recipes

Roasted Rack of Lamb with Macadamia Crust

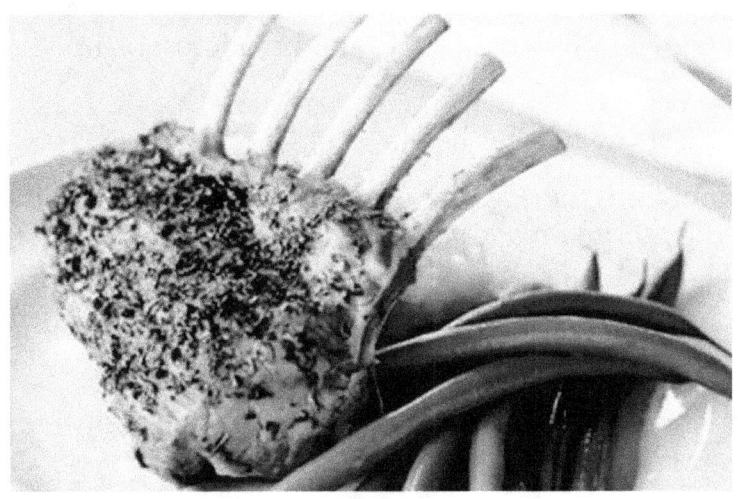

Nutritional Facts/Calories: 215 calories, 16.9g fat, 3.4g carbohydrates, 13.7g protein

Preparation + Cook Time: 45 minutes

Servings: 6

Ingredients:

1 3/4 pound rack of lamb

1 garlic clove (peeled and minced) Salt and pepper to taste

1 tablespoon olive oil For the macadamia crust

3 ounces macadamia nuts (finely chopped) 1 tablespoon breadcrumbs

1 tablespoon fresh rosemary (chopped) 1 egg

Directions/Instructions:

1. Prepare garlic oil. Put olive oil and minced garlic in a bowl and mix well.

2. Brush the meat with garlic oil. Season with salt and pepper.

3. Put the chopped nuts, rosemary, and breadcrumbs in a bowl. Mix well.

4. Whisk the eggs in another bowl.

5. Dip the lamb into the egg mixture. Drain the excess liquid and cover with the macadamia crust. Arrange the coated meat in the cooking basket.

6. Cook for 30 minutes at 220 degrees. Cook for 5 more minutes at 390 degrees.

7. Transfer into a plate and loosely cover with a foil. Leave for 10 minutes to rest before serving.

Barbeque Chicken

Nutritional Facts/Calories: 356 calories, 11g fat, 19.4g carbohydrates, 42.7g protein

Preparation + Cook Time: 40 minutes

Servings: 2

Ingredients:

1 tablespoon molasses

1 tablespoon cider vinegar 1 tablespoon ketchup

2 tablespoons brown sugar 2 chicken thighs

1/4 teaspoon paprika

1/4 teaspoon dry mustard 1/2 teaspoon garlic powder 1/2 teaspoon salt

1/2 teaspoon freshly ground pepper

Directions/Instructions:

1. Put all the ingredients, except the meat in a bowl. Mix well. Soak the meat into the mixture and leave for 30 minutes to marinate.

2. Place the rack in the cooking basket and put the meat on top. Baste the meat with the remaining marinade. Cook for 15 minutes at 380 degrees. Flip the meat, baste with the marinade and cook for 10 more minutes.

Mediterranean Chicken Wings with Olives

Nutritional Facts/Calories: 344 calories, 14.5g fat, 1.4g carbohydrates, 49.4g protein

Preparation + Cook Time: 40 minutes

Servings: 4

Ingredients:

1/2 cup olives

1 1/2 pounds chicken wings 1 teaspoon oregano

1 1/2 teaspoons lemon juice A pinch of salt

A pinch of garlic powder

Directions/Instructions:

1. Mix to combine salt, lemon juice, garlic powder, and oregano in a bowl. Add the meat and toss until coated.

2. Arrange half of the seasoned meat in the cooking basket. Cook for 10 minutes at 356 degrees. Shake the basket twice during the process. Add the olives and cook for 5 more minutes. Perform the same cooking process with the remaining chicken wings.

3. Serve while hot.

Chicken Buffalo Drummies

Nutritional Facts/Calories: 1927 calories, 76.3g fat, 90.2g carbohydrates, 207.9g protein

Preparation + Cook Time: 40 minutes

Servings: 2

Ingredients:

10 chicken drummies (bone-in) 1 cup rice flour

3 cups water

1 cup ice

1 teaspoon cayenne 1/4 cup sugar

1/4 cup salt

For the buffalo sauce

1 teaspoon soy sauce

1 teaspoon cider vinegar 1 teaspoon ketchup

4 tablespoons hot sauce

4 tablespoons melted unsalted butter

Directions/Instructions:

1. Put water, sugar, and salt in a stainless container. Stir until dissolved. Stir in the cayenne pepper. Add the meat and put ice on top. Leave for 2 to 12 hours to brine.

2. Mix to combine all the ingredients for the sauce in a bowl.

3. Remove the meat from the brine mixture and pat them dry. Coat with rice flour and arrange in the cooking basket.

4. Cook for 25 minutes at 400 degrees. Shake the cooking basket twice during the cooking process.

5. Put sauce in a bowl. Add the cooked meat and toss until coated.

Note: You can serve this dish along with carrot or celery sticks. You can also dip the chicken wings on a ranch or blue cheese dressing.

Cornish Hen

Nutritional Facts/Calories: 71 calories, 3.8g fat, 0.7g carbohydrates, 8.6g protein

Preparation + Cook Time: 30 minutes

Servings: 6

Ingredients:

Salt and black pepper to taste 1 fresh lemon (juiced)

Olive oil

1 Cornish hen

Directions/Instructions:

1. Rub the meat with oil and lemon juice. Season with salt and pepper. Tie the hen's legs with a kitchen string.

2. Place in the cooking basket. Cook for 25 minutes at 170 degrees.

Basic Air Fried Chicken

Nutritional Facts/Calories: 575 calories, 22.3g fat, 1.7g carbohydrates, 86.6g protein

Preparation + Cook Time: 50 minutes

Servings: 3

Ingredients:

6 chicken legs (skinless) 1 cup chicken broth

1/4 cup hot sauce 2 teaspoons salt

1 teaspoon garlic powder

1 teaspoon smoked paprika

Directions/Instructions:

1. Mix to combine paprika, garlic powder, salt, hot sauce, and broth in a bowl. Soak the meat and leave to marinate for at least 30 minutes or overnight.

2. Drain the liquid from the meat and pat them dry. Arrange them in the cooking basket. Cook for 17 minutes at 390 degrees.

Black Bean Burger

Nutritional Facts/Calories: 350 calories, 2.6g fat, 64.6g carbohydrates, 19.9g protein

Preparation + Cook Time: 35 minutes

Servings: 6

Ingredients:

1 1/3 cups rolled oats

16 ounces black beans (drained) 3/4 cup salsa

1 tablespoon soy sauce

1 1/4 teaspoons mild chili powder

1/2 teaspoon chipotle chili powder (adjust according to taste) 1/2 teaspoon garlic powder

1/2 cup corn kernels (fresh or frozen/thawed)

Directions/Instructions:

1. Put the oats in a food processor. Pulse up to 6 times or until partially chopped. Add the remaining ingredients, except the corn. Pulse until blended.

2. Transfer the bean mixture to a bowl. Add the corn and mix until combined. Cover the bowl and chill for 15 minutes.

3. Divide the bean mixture into 6 and form them into patties. Arrange in the cooking basket lined with a perforated parchment paper. Lightly spray the patties with oil.

4. Cook for 15 minutes at 375 degrees.

Notes: You can prepare the patties ahead of time. Wrap them before freezing and they will last up to 3 months. Thaw the frozen patties before cooking.

General Tso's Chicken

Nutritional Facts/Calories: 647 calories, 21.6g fat, 40.1g carbohydrates, 68.7g protein

Preparation + Cook Time: 30 minutes

Servings: 4

Ingredients:

1/4 cup water

2 teaspoons cornstarch A pinch of salt

1 teaspoon sesame oil

2 tablespoons rice vinegar

1/2 cup soy sauce 1/2 cup chicken broth 3/4 cup brown sugar

1 teaspoon ginger (minced) 2 teaspoons garlic (minced) 3 green onions (chopped)

6 dried red chilies

1 tablespoon vegetable oil 1/3 cup potato starch

2 pounds chicken thighs (skinless, boneless and chopped into bite-sized pieces)

Directions/Instructions:

1. Coat the meat with potato starch and arrange them in the cooking basket. Cook for 25 minutes at 400 degrees. Shake the basket every 5 minutes during the cooking process.

2. Prepare the sauce. Heat oil in a pan over medium-high flame. Add ginger, garlic, dried chilies, and green onion. Stir for a minute. Add a pinch of salt, sesame oil, rice vinegar, soy sauce, chicken broth, and brown sugar. Bring to a boil. Cook for 3 minutes while frequently stirring.

3. In a bowl, put 1/4 cup of cold water and 2 teaspoons of cornstarch. Mix until dissolved. Add the mixture to the sauce in the pan. Stir and cook for a minute.

4. Serve the meat along with the sauce.

Note: This is best served with vegetables and rice. If you want to create a spicier version, break several pieces on chili peppers in half and add them to the sauce.

Poultry Recipes

Country Chicken Tenders

Nutritional Facts/Calories: 486 calories, 21.6g fat, 29.5g carbohydrates, 41g protein

Preparation + Cook Time: 30 minutes

Servings: 3

Ingredients:

3/4 pound chicken tenders For the breading

1/2 cup seasoned breadcrumbs 2 tablespoons olive oil

2 eggs (beaten)

1 teaspoon black pepper 1/2 teaspoon salt

1/2 cup all-purpose flour

Directions/Instructions:

1. Combine breadcrumbs and salt in a bowl. Add olive oil and mix well.

2. Put the beaten eggs in a different bowl and flour in another.

3. Toss meat in the bowl of flour until coated. Dip them in egg and coat with the breadcrumb mixture. Press using your hands to make the coating stick to the meat. Arrange them in the cooking basket.

4.Cook for 10 minutes at 330 degrees. Turn the temperature to 350 degrees and cook for 5 more minutes.

Buffalo Chicken Tenders

Nutritional Facts/Calories: 380 calories, 12.1g fat, 28g carbohydrates, 41g protein

Preparation + Cook Time: 34 minutes

Servings: 4

Ingredients:

1/2 cup Buffalo sauce 1 cup flour

1 pound chicken tenders (trimmed) 1 cup ranch dressing

1/4 cup blue cheese (crumbled) 1/2 teaspoon garlic powder

1/2 teaspoon cayenne pepper 1/2 teaspoon salt

Directions/Instructions:

1. Put the ranch dressing in a bowl. Add the meat and leave to marinate for an hour.

2. Mix to combine flour, cayenne pepper, salt, and garlic powder in a bowl. Dip each chicken piece in the mixture until coated. Put 2 chicken tenders in the cooking basket at a time

3. Cook for 13 minutes at 400 degrees. Shake the basket twice during the cooking process. Transfer the cooked meat to a bowl and cook the rest.

4. Put the buffalo sauce in a bowl. Add the cooked meat and toss until coated. Transfer to a plate and sprinkle with cheese before serving.

Korean BBQ Satay

Nutritional Facts/Calories: 442 calories, 27.8g fat, 12.6g carbohydrates, 41g protein

Preparation + Cook Time: 22 minutes

Servings: 3

Ingredients:

1 tablespoon grated fresh ginger

2 teaspoons toasted sesame seeds 1/2 cup pineapple juice

1/2 cup low-sodium soy sauce 1/4 cup sesame oil

4 garlic cloves (chopped)

12 ounces chicken tenders (boneless and skinless) 4 scallions (chopped)

A pinch of black pepper

Directions/Instructions:

1. Skewer each piece of meat and trim excess fat.

2. Put the remaining ingredients in a bowl. Mix well. Add the skewered chicken and make sure that all pieces are covered with the mixture. Cover the bowl and refrigerate for 2 hours or overnight.

3. Use paper towels to pat the meat dry. Arrange the skewers in the cooking basket. Cook for 7 minutes at 390 degrees.

Jerk Chicken Wings

Nutritional Facts/Calories: 623 calories, 27.8g fat, 13.6g carbohydrates, 801g protein

Preparation + Cook Time: 33 minutes

Servings: 5

Ingredients:

5 tablespoons lime juice

1 habanero pepper (remove the ribs and seeds, chopped) 1/2 cup red wine vinegar

3 pounds chicken wings 6 garlic cloves (minced) 2 tablespoons soy sauce 2 tablespoons olive oil

1 teaspoon white pepper 1 teaspoon salt

1 teaspoon cinnamon

1 teaspoon cayenne pepper

1 tablespoon grated fresh ginger

1 tablespoon chopped fresh thyme 1 tablespoon allspice

2 tablespoons brown sugar 4 scallions (minced)

Directions/Instructions:

1. Put all ingredients in a bowl and mix until combined and the meat is well-coated. Transfer to a Ziploc bag. Refrigerate for 2 hours or overnight.

2. Drain the liquid and pat the meat dry using paper towels. Arrange them in the cooking basket.

3. Cook for 18 minutes at 390 degrees. Shake the basket halfway through the cooking process.

Note: Serve the dish along with your favorite sauces. You can also try it with ranch dressing or blue cheese dipping sauce.

Fried Chicken Tenders with Mustard and Sage

Nutritional Facts/Calories: 727 calories, 30.9g fat, 21.6g carbohydrates, 85g protein

Preparation + Cook Time: 30 minutes

Servings: 2

Ingredients:

1 tablespoon melted butter 1 tablespoon mayonnaise 1/2 cup panko breadcrumbs 1/2 teaspoon dry sage

4 chicken tenders

1 teaspoon Dijon mustard

Directions/Instructions:

1. Mix to combine sage, mustard, and mayonnaise in a bowl.

2. In another bowl, put the butter and breadcrumbs and mix well.

3. Pat the meat dry using paper towels. Coat each piece with a bit of the mayonnaise mixture and cover with the breadcrumb mixture.

4. Arrange in a single layer in the cooking basket. Cook for 10 minutes at 392 degrees. Flip the meat and cook for 10 more minutes.

Parmesan Crusted Chicken Fillet

Nutritional Facts/Calories: 669 calories, 24g fat, 21.6g carbohydrates, 85g protein

Preparation + Cook Time: 20 minutes

Servings: 4

Ingredients:

1 teaspoon Italian herbs 1 teaspoon garlic powder 1 egg

30 grams salted butter (melted) 1/2 cup parmesan cheese

1 cup panko breadcrumbs

8 pieces chicken tenders or fillet

Directions/Instructions:

1. In a bowl, mix to combine melted butter, egg, Italian herbs, and garlic powder. Add the meat and marinate for at least an hour.

2. Put the Parmesan cheese and panko breadcrumbs in a shallow bowl. Mix until combined.

3. Drain liquid from the meat and coat each piece with the breadcrumb and cheese mixture. Leave for 5 minutes.

4. Line the Air Fryer's base with aluminum foil. Arrange 4 pieces of the coated meat in the basket for each batch. Cook for 6 minutes at 200 degrees. Transfer to a platter and cook the rest of the meat.

5. Serve while hot.

Crispy and Sweet Chicken Wings

Nutritional Facts/Calories: 701 calories, 25g fat, 42.3g carbohydrates, 71g protein

Preparation + Cook Time: 20 minutes

Servings: 6

Ingredients:

1/4 cup all-purpose flour

1/4 cup potato starch or cornstarch 1 egg (large)

1 teaspoon salt

1/2 teaspoon ground red chili pepper

10 chicken wings (remove the tips and slice each wing into 2) 1 tablespoon oil

1/2 cup water or beer

1 fresh ginger (peeled and thinly sliced) 1 1/2 tablespoon soy sauce

1/2 cup dark brown sugar 3 tablespoons rice vinegar 1/2 cup light corn syrup

1/3 cup roasted peanuts (coarsely chopped) 2 tablespoons sesame seeds (toasted)

1 teaspoon red chili flakes

Directions/Instructions:

1. Mix to combine half a teaspoon of ground chili flakes, salt, egg, starch, and flour in a bowl. Put the meat and stir until well-coated.

2. Arrange the 5 pieces of the coated meat in the cooking basket and lightly spray with oil. Cook for 10 minutes at 200 degrees. Transfer to a plate and cook the remaining pieces.

3. Prepare the sauce. Put water in a pot over medium-high flame. Add the corn syrup, vinegar, sugar, soy sauce, and ginger. Bring to a boil. Reduce the heat to low and continue cooking until thick and syrupy. Turn off the heat. Add the cooked chicken, chili flakes, sesame seeds, and peanuts. Mix until combined.

4. Transfer to a bowl and serve immediately.

Chicken Parmesan

Nutritional Facts/Calories: 781 calories, 36g fat, 21.8g carbohydrates, 86.8g protein

Preparation + Cook Time: 30 minutes

Servings: 2

Ingredients:

4 chicken breasts (thinly sliced) 1/2 cup marinara sauce

1/4 cup grated Parmesan cheese 1/3 cup Italian breadcrumbs

2 tablespoons butter (melted) 1/4 cup shredded Mozzarella

Directions/Instructions:

1. Put melted butted in a bowl.

2. Combine Parmesan cheese and breadcrumbs in another bowl.

3. Dip each piece of meat in melted butter and coat with the breadcrumb and cheese mixture. Press using your hands to make the coating stick to the meat.

4. Grease the cooking basket and arrange 2 chicken breasts at a time. Cook for 8 minutes at 400 degrees.

5. Sprinkle the half cooked meat with a tablespoon of mozzarella cheese and drizzle with a tablespoon of marinara sauce. Cook for 5 more minutes at 370 degrees.

Notes: You can serve the dish along with fresh salad. You can also substitute butter with olive oil.

Pork Recipes

Pizza Rolls

Nutritional Facts/Calories: 170 calories, 10g fat, 12.9g carbohydrates, 9g protein

Preparation + Cook Time: 50 minutes

Servings: 6

Ingredients:

1 14-ounce jar of pizza sauce

2 pieces of Italian sausage (cooked and crumbled) 1 onion (chopped)

15 eggroll wrappers

2 cups shredded mozzarella cheese 2 red peppers (roasted and chopped) 3 ounces sliced pepperoni (chopped) 1 teaspoon garlic powder

Directions/Instructions:

1. Mix to combine the peppers, cheese, onions, pepperoni, and sausage in a bowl. Add the garlic powder and pizza sauce. Mix well. Scoop 1/4 of the mixture to each eggroll wrapper. Fold all sides until the filling is wrapped. Moisten the last fold to secure. Roll it tightly.

Perform the same steps with the rest of the wrappers. Put in a container, cover and freeze overnight.

2. Arrange 5 rolls in the cooking basket at a time and lightly spray them with a non-stick cooking spray. Cook for 7 minutes at 400 degrees and cook for 7 minutes. Flip the pizza rolls and cook for 2 more minutes. Transfer to a platter and cook the remaining rolls.

3. Serve the rolls with pizza sauce for dipping.

Pigs in a Blanket

Nutritional Facts/Calories: 513 calories, 34.5g fat, 31.8g carbohydrates, 17.9g protein

Preparation + Cook Time: 31 minutes

Servings: 4

Ingredients:

1 8-ounce can of crescent rolls

1 12-ounce package of cocktail franks

Directions/Instructions:

1. Drain the liquid from the cocktail franks. Use paper towels to pat them dry.

2. Cut the dough into strips. Roll each strip into a piece of the frank. Leave the edges visible. Chill for 5 minutes or until firm.

3. Arrange the wrapped cocktail franks in the cooking basket. Cook for 8 minutes at 330 degrees. Turn the temperature setting to 390 degrees and cook for 3 more minutes.

Bacon Wrapped Dates with Blue Cheese

Nutritional Facts/Calories: 174 calories, 10.8g fat, 11g carbohydrates, 9.1g protein

Preparation + Cook Time: 28 minutes

Servings: 6

Ingredients:

1 teaspoon Cajun seasoning

1/4 pound blue cheese (cut into 10) 10 Medjool dates (pitted)

4 bacon strips (cut into 3)

Directions/Instructions:

1. Insert blue cheese inside each date. Wrap the filled dates with bacon. Secure its hold with a toothpick. Arrange them in the cooking basket.

2. Cook for 5 minutes at 400 degrees. Flip the dates and cook for 3 more minutes.

3. Transfer to a platter and sprinkle with Cajun seasoning before serving.

Asian Style Baby Back Ribs

Nutritional Facts/Calories: 346 calories, 27g fat, 15g carbohydrates, 9.1g protein

Preparation + Cook Time: 1 hour 15 minutes

Servings: 2

Ingredients:

2 tablespoons sesame oil

1 jalapeño (seeded and chopped) 1/2 tablespoon chopped cilantro 1 slab baby back ribs

1 scallion (finely chopped) 1 cup orange juice

1 teaspoon grated ginger 1 garlic clove (minced)

Directions/Instructions:

1. Put all the ingredients in a Ziploc bag and seal. Shake until all sides of the meat are coated. Refrigerate overnight to marinate.

2. Reserve the marinade. Arrange the ribs in the cooking basket in a vertical position. Cook for 35 minutes at 350 degrees.

3. Pour the marinade in a pan over medium-high flame. Cook until the liquid is reduced by half. Turn off the stove.

4. Brush the half-cooked ribs with the marinade and cook for 30 more minutes.

5. Transfer to a plate and slice. Serve along with the remaining marinade.

Tortilla Crusted Pork Loin Chops

Nutritional Facts/Calories: 463 calories, 27g fat, 32g carbohydrates, 25.1g protein

Preparation + Cook Time: 30 minutes

Servings: 2

Ingredients:

1 teaspoon sauce (hot sauce, steak sauce or Worcestershire sauce)

1/2 teaspoon salt

2 pork loin chops (boneless) 1 egg (beaten)

1/2 cup buttermilk

1/2 cup crushed tortilla chips 1/2 cup flour

Directions/Instructions:

1. Put salt, Worcestershire sauce, and buttermilk in a Ziploc bag. Seal and shake until combined. Add the meat and shake until all sides are coated. Refrigerate overnight to marinate.

2. Drain liquid from the meat and use paper towels to pat excess liquid.

3. Put the beaten egg in a bowl, crushed chips in another bowl, and the flour in a different bowl.

4. Coat the meat with flour, dip in the egg and press into the crushed chips until all sides are covered. Arrange them in the cooking basket.

5. Cook for 15 minutes at 356 degrees. Flip the meat halfway through the cooking process.

6. Transfer to a plate and leave to rest for 5 minutes before serving.

Cheddar Bacon Croquettes

Nutritional Facts/Calories: 962 calories, 68.6g fat, 32g carbohydrates, 53.1g protein

Preparation + Cook Time: 28 minutes

Servings: 6

Ingredients:

For the breading

4 tablespoons olive oil 1 cup all-purpose flour

1 cup seasoned breadcrumbs 2 eggs (beaten)

For the filling

1 pound bacon slices

1 pound sharp cheddar cheese

Directions/Instructions:

1. Cut the cheese into 6 equal portions. Wrap each piece with 2 bacon slices. Trim excess fat. Chill for 5 minutes.

2. In a shallow bowl, mix the breadcrumbs and oil.

3. Dip each bacon wrapped cheese in the flour, cover with eggs and roll in the breadcrumbs mixture. Arrange in the cooking basket.

4. Cook for 8 minutes at 390 degrees.

Jalapeno Bacon Poppers

Nutritional Facts/Calories: 463 calories, 31.6g fat, 9.1g carbohydrates, 35g protein

Preparation + Cook Time: 40 minutes

Servings: 4

Ingredients:

12 bacon slices (thin)

1/4 teaspoon black pepper 1/4 teaspoon sea salt

3 green onions (minced)

1/2 cup sharp white cheddar cheese (freshly shredded) 2 tablespoons Greek Yogurt

12 jalapeno peppers (large)

Directions/Instructions:

1. Place each pepper in a chopping board and cut into 2 in a lengthwise manner. Remove the membranes and seeds.

2. Put the black pepper, salt, green onion, cheddar cheese, and yogurt in a blender. Process until smooth. Transfer to a bowl, cover, and refrigerate until firm.

3. Scoop a small portion of the filling in the half part of a pepper and place the top part on top to enclose the filling. Wrap each filled pepper with a slice of bacon and secure it with a toothpick.

4. Arrange them in the cooking basket. Cook for 15 minutes at 400 degrees.

Jamaican Jerk Pork

Nutritional Facts/Calories: 338 calories, 12g fat, 1.1g carbohydrates, 53g protein

Preparation + Cook Time: 30 minutes

Servings: 4

Ingredients:

1/4 cup jerk paste

1.5 pounds pork butt (chopped into 3 chunks)

Directions/Instructions:

1. Rub meat with the jerk paste. Refrigerate for at least 4 hours or overnight to marinate. Leave at a room temperature for 20 minutes before cooking.

2. Spray the bottom part of the cooking basket with oil before putting the marinated meat. Cook for 20 minutes at 390 degrees. Flip the meat halfway through the cooking process.

3. Transfer to a platter and leave for 10 minutes to rest before serving.

Beef recipes

Fried Meatballs in Tomato Sauce

Nutritional Facts/Calories: 436 calories, 14g fat, 10.8g carbohydrates, 63.6g protein

Preparation + Cook Time: 25 minutes

Servings: 4

Ingredients:

3/4 pound ground beef Salt and pepper to taste

1 tablespoon chopped parsley

1/2 tablespoon fresh thyme leaves (chopped) 10 ounces tomato sauce

1 egg

1 onion (chopped)

3 tablespoons breadcrumbs

Directions/Instructions:

1. Put all the ingredients in a bowl and mix until combined. Use your hands to form 12 small balls from the mixture. Arrange them in the cooking basket.

2. Cook for 8 minutes at 390 degrees. Transfer the meatballs to an oven dish. Drizzle with tomato sauce on top.

3. Place the oven dish in the cooking basket and cook for 5 minutes at 330 degrees.

Mini Cheeseburger Sliders

Nutritional Facts/Calories: 555 calories, 28g fat, 9.1g carbohydrates, 61g protein

Preparation + Cook Time: 19 minutes

Servings: 3

Ingredients:

6 slices of cheddar cheese Salt and black pepper to taste 1 pound ground beef

6 dinner rolls

Directions/Instructions:

1. Divide the meat into 6 and form them into patties. Season with salt and pepper.

2. Arrange the patties in the cooking basket. Cook for 10 minutes at 390 degrees. Place cheese on top of each patty and continue cooking for a minute.

3. Fill each dinner roll with the cooked patty.

Chimichurri Skirt Steak

Nutritional Facts/Calories: 1175 calories, 100.3gfat, 10.6g carbohydrates, 61g protein

Preparation + Cook Time: 25 minutes

Servings: 2

Ingredients:

1 pound skirt steak For the chimichurri

3 garlic cloves (minced)

1/4 cup finely chopped mint 1 tablespoon ground cumin 3/4 cup olive oil

1/4 teaspoon black pepper

2 tablespoons minced oregano 1 cup chopped parsley

1 teaspoon cayenne pepper

1 teaspoon crushed red pepper 1 teaspoon salt

3tablespoons red wine vinegar 2 teaspoons smoked paprika

Directions/Instructions:

1. Put all the ingredients for the chimichurri in a bowl. Mix well. Pour 1/4 cup of the mixture to a Ziploc bag.

2. Slice the steak into 2. Put them in a Ziploc bag along with the chimichurri. Seal the bag and shake until all sides of the meat are coated. Refrigerate for at least 2 hours or overnight.

3. Leave the marinated meat at room temperature half an hour before cooking. Drain the liquid and pat the meat with paper towels to dry.

4. Arrange the meat in the cooking basket. Cook for 10 minutes at 390 degrees for a medium-rare steak. Add more minutes if you want it well done.

5. Transfer to a platter and drizzle with 2 tablespoons of chimichurri before serving.

Stuffed Peppers

Nutritional Facts/Calories: 515 calories, 29g fat, 13.6g carbohydrates, 50g protein

Preparation + Cook Time: 30 minutes

Servings: 2

Ingredients:

4 ounces cheddar cheese (shredded) 1/2 teaspoon black pepper

1/2 teaspoon salt

1 teaspoon Worcestershire sauce 1/2 cup tomato sauce

8 ounces lean ground beef 1 teaspoon olive oil

1 garlic clove (minced)

1/2 medium onion (chopped)

2 medium green peppers (remove seeds and stems)

Directions/Instructions:

1. Put water and salt in a pan over medium-high flame and bring to a boil. Reduce heat to medium, put the peppers and cook for 3 minutes.

2. Heat olive oil in a pan skillet over medium flame. Add garlic and onion and saute until golden. Remove from heat.

3. Transfer the cooked garlic and onion in a bowl. Add half of the shredded cheese, Worcestershire sauce, 1/4 cup tomato sauce, and beef. Season with salt and pepper and mix well. Stuff the pepper halves with the filling. Put the rest of the tomato sauce on top and add cheese.

4. Arrange in the cooking basket. Cook for 20 minutes at 390 degrees.

Steak with Garlic Herb Butter

Nutritional Facts/Calories: 1905 calories, 89g fat, 1.7g carbohydrates, 250g protein

Preparation + Cook Time: 32 minutes

Servings: 2

Ingredients:

1/2 teaspoon salt

1 teaspoon Worcestershire sauce 2 teaspoons garlic minced

2 tablespoons fresh parsley (chopped) 1 stick unsalted butter (softened) Garlic butter

Olive oil

Black pepper (freshly cracked) 2 8-ounce ribeye steak

Directions/Instructions:

1. Prepare the garlic butter. Put Worcestershire sauce, garlic, parsley, and butter in a bowl. Mix well. Season with salt. Transfer to a parchment paper and roll like a log. Chill until ready to cook.

2. Rub all sides of the steak with olive oil. Season with black pepper and salt.

3. Grease the fryer's cooking basket before placing the meat. Cook for 12 minutes in a preheated Air Fryer at 400 degrees. Flip the meat halfway through the cooking process.

4. Transfer to a plate and leave to rest for 5 minutes. Add garlic butter on top before serving.

Notes: You can skip rubbing the meat with olive oil if preferred. The oil adds flavor to the meat. You can adjust the time of the cooking process depending on how you want your meat to be done. This recipe cooks medium done steak. Adjust the time to 10 minutes if you want it medium rare and 14 minutes for medium well.

Meatloaf

Nutritional Facts/Calories: 290 calories, 8.9g fat, 10.7g carbohydrates, 36g protein

Preparation + Cook Time: 50 minutes

Servings: 8

Ingredients:

2 pounds ground beef 1/2 teaspoon kosher salt

1 tablespoon Worcestershire sauce 1 tablespoon Dijon style mustard

3 tablespoons ketchup 2 eggs (lightly beaten) 2 garlic cloves

1/2 cup onions (chopped) 1/2 cup carrots (shredded)

1/2 cup mushrooms (chopped) 1/4 cup beef broth

1 cup fresh soft bread crumbs For the glaze

2 teaspoons Dijon mustard 1/4 cup brown sugar

1/2 cup ketchup

Directions/Instructions:

1. Mix beef broth and breadcrumbs in a bowl. Set aside.

2. Put garlic, onions, carrots, and mushrooms in a food processor. Process until finely chopped. Transfer to a bowl. Add meat, Worcestershire sauce, Dijon mustard, ketchup, and the broth and breadcrumb mixture. Mix well. Season with salt. Use your hands to combine all ingredients and shape the mixture into a loaf.

3. Place the meatloaf in a greased cooking basket. Cook for 45 minutes in a preheated Air Fryer at 390 degrees.

4. Prepare the glaze. Combine all ingredients for the glaze in a bowl. Open the cooking basket of the Air Fryer 5 minutes before the cooking process is done. Brush glaze all over the meatloaf and continue cooking.

5. Transfer meatloaf to a plate. Leave to rest for 10 minutes before serving.

Seafood Recipes

Crab Croquettes

Nutritional Facts/Calories: 322 calories, 18.3g fat, 34.1g carbohydrates, 20g protein

Preparation + Cook Time: 30 minutes

Servings: 6

Ingredients:

1/4 cup red onion (finely chopped) 1/4 cup sour cream

1/4 cup mayonnaise

1/2 teaspoon cayenne pepper

1/2 teaspoon parsley (finely chopped) 1 tablespoon olive oil

2 tablespoons celery (finely chopped) 2 egg whites (beaten)

1 pound of lump crab meat 1/4 red bell pepper (chopped)

1/4 teaspoon chives (finely chopped) 1/4 teaspoon tarragon

For the breading

3 eggs (beaten)

1 teaspoon olive oil

1 cup panko breadcrumbs 1 cup all-purpose flour

1/2 teaspoon salt

Directions/Instructions:

1. Heat oil in a pan over medium-high flame. Add the onions, celery, and peppers. Saute for 5 minutes. Remove from heat and set aside.

2. Put the breadcrumbs, salt, and olive oil in a food processor. Process until fine.

3. Put the flour, panko mixture, and eggs in 3 separate bowls.

4. Put the crabmeat, mayonnaise, egg whites, spices, vegetables, and sour cream in a bowl and mix until combined. Use your hands to shape them into golf-size crabmeat balls.

5. Roll each ball into the flour, eggs, and panko mixture. Press the coating to make them stick.

6. Arrange them in the cooking basket. Cook for 10 minutes at 390 degrees.

Cod Fish Nuggets

Nutritional Facts/Calories: 404 calories, 11.6g fat, 38.6g carbohydrates, 34.6g protein

Preparation + Cook Time: 25 minutes

Servings: 4

Ingredients:

1 pound of cod (cut into strips) For the breading

2 eggs (beaten)

3/4 cup breadcrumbs 1 cup all-purpose flour 2 tablespoons olive oil A pinch of salt

Directions/Instructions:

1. Put olive oil, salt, and panko breadcrumbs in a food processor. Process until fine. Transfer mixture to a bowl.

2. Put the flour and the beaten eggs in separate bowls.

3. Coat each cod strip with flour. Dip in the eggs and coat with breadcrumbs. Press the coating to make it stick.

4. Arrange the coated cod pieces in the cooking basket. Cook for 10 minutes at 390 degrees.

Fish Tacos

Nutritional Facts/Calories: 618 calories, 17g fat, 71.7g carbohydrates, 36g protein

Preparation + Cook Time: 17 minutes

Servings: 4

Ingredients:

2 snapper or grouper fillets 1 egg

1 cup plain breadcrumbs 1 cup panko breadcrumbs 6 taco shells (premade)

1 cup salsa

1 cup shredded lettuce

1 cup, plus 1/2 cup of sour cream 1/2 cup medium salsa

1/2 cup shredded low-fat cheddar cheese 1/2 cup buttermilk

1/4 cup flour

1/4 teaspoon black pepper 1/2 teaspoon garlic powder 1/2 teaspoon salt

Directions/Instructions:

1.   Put the flour, egg, and buttermilk in a bowl. Mix well until combined. Set aside.

2.   Put the breadcrumbs, black pepper, salt, and garlic powder in a shallow dish and mix well.

3.   Dip the fillets in the egg mixture and coat each piece with the breadcrumbs mixture.

4.   Arrange the coated fillets in the cooking basket and lightly spray with oil. Cook for 12 minutes at 400 degrees.

5.   Put cheese, sour cream, salsa, and lettuce in taco shells and top with the cooked fillets.

Fish with Chips

Nutritional Facts/Calories: 646 calories, 33g fat, 48g carbohydrates, 41g protein

Preparation + Cook Time: 22 minutes

Servings: 2

Ingredients:

1 cod fillet (6 ounces)

3 cups salt

3 cups vinegar-flavored kettle cooked chips 1/4 cup buttermilk

1/4 teaspoon pepper 1/2 teaspoon salt

Directions/Instructions:

1. Mix to combine the buttermilk, pepper, and salt in a bowl. Put the cod and leave to soak for 5 minutes.

2. Put the chips in a food processor and process until crushed. Transfer to a shallow bowl. Coat the fillet with the crushed chips.

3. Put the coated fillet in the cooking basket. Cook for 12 minutes at 400 degrees.

Tuna Melt Sandwich

Nutritional Facts/Calories: 261 calories, 8.43g fat, 27.15g carbohydrates, 22.46g protein

Preparation + Cook Time: 21 minutes

Servings: 2

Ingredients:

1 celery stalk (finely chopped)

1/2 cup shredded sharp cheddar cheese 1/8 teaspoon celery salt

1 teaspoon onion (finely chopped) A pinch of black pepper

1 5-ounce can of solid white tuna in water (drained) 2 slices of bread (multi-grain)

2 tablespoons mayonnaise 4 slices of ripe tomato

Directions/Instructions:

1. Put the bread slices in the cooking basket. Cook for 3 minutes at 400 degrees.

2. In a bowl, mix to combine the mayonnaise, tuna, salt, pepper, onion, and celery. Spread the mixture in the 2 toasted bread slices. Add 2 tomato slices and cheese on top of each bread slice.

3. Put one sandwich in the cooking basket at a time. Cook for 4 minutes at 400 degrees. Repeat the same step with the other sandwich

Salmon with Dill Sauce

Nutritional Facts/Calories: 348 calories, 18.97g fat, 5.29g carbohydrates, 37.694g protein

Preparation + Cook Time: 45 minutes

Servings: 4

Ingredients:

2 teaspoons olive oil

4 6-ounce pieces of salmon A pinch of salt

For the dill sauce

1/2 cup sour cream

1/2 cup Greek yogurt (non-fat)

2 tablespoons finely chopped dill A pinch of salt

Directions/Instructions:

1. Drizzle each piece of salmon with olive oil. Season with salt. Put them in the cooking basket. Cook for 30 minutes at 270 degrees.

2. Prepare the sauce. Combine all the ingredients for the sauce in a bowl. Mix well.

3. Serve the fish with the sauce. Top with chopped dill.

Cajun Shrimp

Nutritional Facts/Calories: 173 calories, 5.35g fat, 0.21g carbohydrates, 28.99g protein

Preparation + Cook Time: 10 minutes

Servings: 4

Ingredients:

1/2 teaspoon old bay seasoning 1 tablespoon olive oil

1 1/4 pounds tiger shrimp A pinch of salt

1/4 teaspoon smoked paprika 1/4 teaspoon cayenne pepper

Directions/Instructions:

1. Mix to combine all the ingredients in a bowl until all the shrimp pieces are coated with the spices and oil.

2. Arrange them in the cooking basket. Cook for 5 minutes at 390 degrees.

Note: The dish is best eaten with rice.

Banging Shrimp

Nutritional Facts/Calories: 263 calories, 9.99g fat, 13.12g carbohydrates, 28.25g protein

Preparation + Cook Time: 40 minutes

Servings: 4

Ingredients:

1 teaspoon salt

1 egg (beaten)

1 pound jumbo shrimp (peeled and deveined) 2 tablespoons all-purpose flour

2 tablespoons cornstarch 1/2 teaspoon garlic powder 1/2 teaspoon paprika

1/2 teaspoon Sriracha

1/2 teaspoon cayenne pepper 1/2 teaspoon sugar

1/2 cup panko breadcrumbs 1/2 cup milk

For the dipping sauce

1 tablespoon ketchup

1 teaspoon Sriracha 1/4 cup mayonnaise

Directions/Instructions:

1. Put all the ingredients, except for the shrimp and breadcrumbs, in a shallow baking dish. Mix well.

2, Put the breadcrumbs in another baking dish.

3. Dip the shrimp in the batter mixture and coat with panko breadcrumbs.

4. Arrange 6 pieces of coated shrimps in the cooking basket at a time and lightly spray with oil. Cook for 10 minutes at 400 degrees. Shake the basket halfway during the cooking process.

5. Transfer to a plate and cook the rest of the shrimp.

6. Prepare the sauce. Put all the ingredients for the sauce in a bowl and mix until combined.

7. Put the cooked shrimp in the sauce and toss until coated. Transfer to a plate and serve along with shredded lettuce.

Coconut Shrimp

Nutritional Facts/Calories: 239 calories, 8.67g fat, 22.05g carbohydrates, 16.69g protein

Preparation + Cook Time: 28 minutes

Servings: 4

Ingredients:

1 tablespoon water 1/2 teaspoon salt

1/3 cup panko breadcrumbs

1/2 pound jumbo shrimp (peeled and deveined) 2 eggs

1/2 cup sweetened coconut flakes 1/2 cup cornstarch

Directions/Instructions:

1.   Beat egg and water in a shallow baking dish. Mix the coconut flakes, breadcrumbs, and salt in another baking dish.

2.   Put the cornstarch and shrimp in a zip bag. Shake until evenly coated. Dip each piece of shrimp in the egg mixture and coat with the breadcrumb mixture. Arrange 6 coated shrimp in the cooking basket of the Air Fryer at a time. Set to 400 degrees and cook for 6 minutes. Transfer to a platter and cook the rest of the shrimp.

Teriyaki Glazed Halibut Steak

Nutritional Facts/Calories: 374 calories, 21.22g fat, 18.12g carbohydrates, 27.82g protein

Preparation + Cook Time: 52 minutes

Servings: 3

Ingredients:

1 pound halibut steak For the marinade

1/4 cup orange juice 1/4 cup sugar

1/2 cup mirin

2 tablespoons lime juice 1 garlic clove (smashed)

2/3 cup low-sodium soy sauce 1/4 teaspoon ground ginger

1/4 teaspoon red pepper flakes (crushed)

Directions/Instructions:

1. Put all the ingredients for the marinade in a pan over medium flame. Bring to a boil while stirring often. Set aside to cool.

2. Transfer half of the marinade in a Ziploc bag. Add the halibut steak and seal. Chill for at least half an hour.

3. Place the marinated halibut steak in the cooking basket. Cook for 12 minutes at 390 degrees.

4. Brush the remaining marinade over the steak before serving.

Note: This is best served with rice.

Cajun Style Fried Shrimp

Nutritional Facts/Calories: 295 calories, 4.11g fat, 44.11g carbohydrates, 18.38g protein

Preparation + Cook Time: 45 minutes

Servings: 4

Ingredients:

1 cup cornmeal

1/8 teaspoon pepper

1/2 teaspoon garlic powder 1 egg

1/2 pound jumbo shrimp (peeled and deveined) 1/4 teaspoon dried oregano

1/4 teaspoon dried leaf thyme 1/2 cup all-purpose flour

1 teaspoon cayenne

1 teaspoon salt

Directions/Instructions:

1. Soak the shrimp in a bowl with cold water. Drain liquid and use paper towels to pat the shrimp dry.

2. In another bowl, whisk the egg, garlic powder, salt, black pepper, cayenne, oregano, and thyme.

3. Spread flour in a sheet of wax paper and the cornmeal in another.

4. Dredge the shrimp in flour. Dip each piece in the egg mixture and coat with cornmeal.

5. Put 6 pieces of the coated shrimp in the cooking basket at a time. Lightly spray them with oil. Cook for 10 minutes at 400 degrees. Transfer to a platter and cook the remaining shrimp.

Cod Fingers

Nutritional Facts/Calories: 523 calories, 6.83g fat, 80.16g carbohydrates, 31.32g protein

Preparation + Cook Time: 55 minutes

Servings: 4

Ingredients:

1 pound of cod (sliced into 2-inch strips) 1 cup all-purpose flour

2 eggs

1 cup yellow cornmeal 1 cup instant flour

2 tablespoons milk

1 teaspoon salt

1 teaspoon seafood seasoning

Directions/Instructions:

1. Whisk the egg and milk in a shallow bowl.

2. In another bowl, combine the cornmeal, salt, and flour.

3. Put the seafood seasoning and instant flour in a Ziploc bag. Shake until combined. Add the cod and gently shake until all sides are coated.

4. Dip the cod to the egg mixture and coat with the cornmeal mixture. Arrange 2 pieces of coated cod in the cooking basket at a time.

5. Cook for 10 minutes at 400 degrees. Transfer to a platter and cook the remaining pieces of cod.

Note: You can serve the dish with tartar sauce and garnish it with lemon slices.

Sesame Encrusted Ahi Tuna with Hoisin Sauce

Nutritional Facts/Calories: 767 calories, 51.62g fat, 18.98g carbohydrates, 57.59g protein

Preparation + Cook Time: 55 minutes

Servings: 2

Ingredients:

1/4 teaspoon freshly ground pepper 1 egg white (beaten)

2 ahi tuna steaks (around 1.5 inches thick) 1 tablespoon black sesame seeds

1/4 cup sesame seeds 1/2 teaspoon salt

For the sauce

1/4 cup Hoisin sauce

1/4 teaspoon ground white pepper Juice of 2 limes

1 tablespoon honey

2 tablespoons low-sodium soy sauce 2 tablespoons rice wine vinegar

Directions/Instructions:

1. Whisk all the ingredients for the sauce in a bowl. Set aside.

2. Mix to combine sesame seeds, pepper, and salt in a shallow bowl.

3. Beat the egg white in a different bowl.

4. Dip the tuna steaks in the beaten egg white and coat each piece with the seasoned sesame seeds. Gently press to make the coating stick.

5. Arrange the coated tuna steaks in the cooking basket. Cook for 3 minutes at 400 degrees. Flip and cook for 3 more minutes.

6. Slice the steaks and serve with the sauce on the side.

Crab Cakes

Nutritional Facts/Calories: 303 calories, 15.61g fat, 28.39g carbohydrates, 13.22g protein

Preparation + Cook Time: 52 minutes

Servings: 4

Ingredients:

6 pieces butter crackers (crushed) Black pepper to taste

1/2 teaspoon salt

1/2 teaspoon garlic powder 1 tablespoon corn flour

1 tablespoon mayonnaise

3 stalks spring onions (chopped) 1 yellow onion (chopped)

1 egg

500 grams frozen crab meat (thawed)

Directions/Instructions:

1. Bring water to a boil and remove from heat.

2. Soak the crab meat in boiling water for a couple of seconds. Drain excess moist and place on a plate lined with paper towels.

3. Put the crab meat in a bowl. Add the rest of the ingredients. Mix until combined. Use your hands to form the mixture into your desired shapes and sizes.

4. Arrange the crab cakes in the cooking basket. Cook for 10 minutes at 350 degrees.

Vegetable Recipes

Stuffed Garlic Mushrooms

Nutritional Facts/Calories: 89 calories, 5.58g fat, 7.63g carbohydrates, 3.48g protein

Preparation + Cook Time: 23 minutes

Servings: 4

Ingredients:

16 button mushrooms For the stuffing

1 1/2 slices of white bread

1 tablespoon flat-leafed parsley (minced) 1 garlic clove (crushed)

1 1/2 tablespoons olive oil Ground black pepper

Directions/Instructions:

1. Put the bread slices in a food processor and process into fine crumbs. Add pepper, parsley, and garlic. Process until combined. Transfer to a bowl. Add olive oil and mix well.

2. Chop of the mushroom stalks. Scoop the crumb mixture into the mushroom caps and pat using your hands to make them stick.

3. Arrange the mushroom caps in the cooking basket. Cook for 8 minutes at 390 degrees.

Mushroom, Onion and Feta Frittata

Nutritional Facts/Calories: 352 calories, 26.42g fat, 9.22g carbohydrates, 20.47g protein

Preparation + Cook Time: 29 minutes

Servings: 4

Ingredients:

4 cups button mushrooms (rinsed and thinly sliced) 2 tablespoons olive oil

1 red onion (peeled and thinly sliced) 6 tablespoons crumbled feta cheese 6 eggs

A pinch of salt

Directions/Instructions:

1. Heat oil in a pan over medium flame. Cook the onions and mushrooms for 3 minutes. Transfer to a bowl and set aside.

2. Whisk the eggs and a pinch of salt in a bowl. Transfer to a lightly greased baking dish. Add the cooked mushroom, onion, and cheese.

3. Place the rack in the cooking basket and put the baking dish on top. Cook for 30 minutes at 330 degrees.

Asparagus Frittata

Nutritional Facts/Calories: 320 calories, 21.59g fat, 9.1g carbohydrates, 21.59g protein

Preparation + Cook Time: 20 minutes Servings: 1

Ingredients:

2 tablespoons milk

2 eggs

Salt and pepper to taste

1 tablespoon Parmesan cheese (freshly grated) 5 asparagus tips (steamed)

Directions/Instructions:

1. Whisk the eggs, milk, salt, pepper, and cheese in a bowl until combined. Transfer to a greased baking dish. Put the steamed asparagus on top.

2. Place the rack inside the cooking basket and put the baking dish on top. Cook for 5 minutes at 400 degrees.

Fried Green Tomatoes

Nutritional Facts/Calories: 249 calories, 2.24g fat, 46.95g carbohydrates, 10.63g protein

Preparation + Cook Time: 25 minutes

Servings: 2

Ingredients:

1 teaspoon salt

1/2 tablespoon Creole seasoning 1/2 teaspoon pepper

2 green tomatoes

1 cup buttermilk

1 cup panko breadcrumbs

1/2 cup instant flour

Directions/Instructions:

1. Slice the tomatoes to 1/4-inch thickness. Season both sides with salt and pepper.

2. Put the buttermilk and flour in 2 different bowls.

3. Mix the Creole seasoning and panko crumbs in another bowl.

4. Dredge each slice of tomato in the flour. Soak it in the buttermilk and coat with the panko mixture. Gently press the coating using your hands to make them stick.

5. Put the rack in the cooking basket and arrange 3 coated tomato slices on top of the rack. Lightly spray them with oil. Cook for 5 minutes at 400 degrees. Transfer to a plate and cook the remaining tomato slices.

6. Sprinkle the cooked tomatoes with your preferred amount of Creole seasoning.

Note: You can serve the dish along with a ranch dressing.

Crusty Potato Wedges

Nutritional Facts/Calories: 207 calories, 4.39g fat, 34.71g carbohydrates, 8.05g protein

Preparation + Cook Time: 35 minutes

Servings: 4

Ingredients:

1 teaspoon dried thyme 1 teaspoon garlic powder

1/4 cup grated Parmesan cheese 1/2 tablespoon dried rosemary

2 potatoes (sliced into wedges) 1/2 teaspoon paprika

1/2 teaspoon salt 1/2 teaspoon pepper 1 egg (beaten)

Directions/Instructions:

1. In a bowl, mix to combine the Parmesan cheese, rosemary, garlic powder, salt, pepper, thyme, and paprika.

2. Dip the potato wedges in the beaten egg. Put them in the spiced cheese mixture and toss until coated.

3. Arrange the coated potato wedges in the cooking basket. Lightly spray them with oil. Cook for 20 minutes at 400 degrees. Shake the basket twice during the cooking duration.

Noodley Kebabs

Nutritional Facts/Calories: 383 calories, 28.16g fat, 31.65g carbohydrates, 4.12g protein

Preparation + Cook Time: 1 hour 10 minutes

Servings: 4

Ingredients:

2 bread slices (turned into breadcrumbs) 1/2 teaspoon soy sauce

1 tablespoon coriander (chopped) 2 potatoes (boiled and grated)

1 onion

1/2 cup mixed vegetables (partially boiled) 2 teaspoons chopped ginger

2 green chilies

Red chili powder to taste Salt to taste

For Coating

3/4 cup noodles (boiled) Milk

Directions/Instructions:

1. In a bowl, mix to combine mixed veggies, grated potatoes, salt, green chilies, soy sauce, and ginger. Use your hands to shape themixture into small oval croquettes.

2. Dip each croquette in milk and wrap with the boiled noodles.

2. Arrange them in the cooking basket. Cook for 30 minutes at 350 degrees. Flip them halfway through the cooking process.

3. Serve while hot with tomato sauce on the side.

Vegetable Croquettes

Nutritional Facts/Calories: 197 calories, 5.98g fat, 35.03g carbohydrates, 3.97g protein

Preparation + Cook Time: 1 hour 10 minutes

Servings: 6

Ingredients:

2 green chilies (finely chopped) 1 onion (chopped)

1 tablespoon olive oil

1 tablespoon grated cabbage Salt and pepper to taste

1   carrot (grated)

2   potatoes (boiled and grated) 1 cup white breadcrumbs

1 1/2 cups dry breadcrumbs

3 tablespoons dry maida (for coating)

1 capsicum (minced) For the white sauce

1/4 teaspoon dried parsley 1/4 teaspoon dried oregano 1/4 teaspoon dried basil Salt and pepper to taste 1/2 cup milk

1 tablespoon maida

1 tablespoon butter

For corn flour solution

3 tablespoons of corn flour (mixed with 1 cup of water)

Directions/Instructions:

1. Prepare the sauce. Melt butter in a pan over medium flame. Stir in 1 tablespoon of maida. Mix until frothy. Reduce the heat to low and stir in the milk. Season with salt, pepper, and other seasonings. Remove from heat.

2. Heat oil in another pan over medium-high flame. Saute the green chilies and onion for 3 minutes. Stir in the capsicums, salt, cabbage, and carrot. Cook for 5 minutes while stirring often. Transfer to a bowl. Add the boiled potatoes and season with salt. Add the white breadcrumbs and white sauce. Mix until well-combined. Use your hands to turn the mixture into croquettes.

3. Dip the croquettes in the corn flour solution and roll them in the dry maida until coated. Drizzle with the corn flour solution and coat with dry breadcrumbs. Use your hands to press the coating to make them stick.

4. Transfer the coated croquettes to a platter and cover with a cling wrap. Freeze until ready to use.

5. Arrange the croquettes in the cooking basket. Cook for 30 minutes at 356 degrees. Flip them halfway through the cooking process.

Marinated Artichoke Hearts

Nutritional Facts/Calories: 79 calories, 3.55g fat, 11.04g carbohydrates, 3.18g protein

Preparation + Cook Time: 15 minutes

Servings: 4

Ingredients:

12 ounces artichoke hearts (frozen)

Salt, garlic powder, black pepper, and red pepper flakes to taste 1 teaspoon oregano

1 tablespoon olive oil

1 tablespoon lemon juice 1/2 teaspoon thyme

Directions/Instructions:

1. Mix to combine olive oil, salt, pepper, lemon juice, garlic powder, thyme, and oregano in a bowl. Add the artichokes and toss until coated. Arrange them in the cooking basket. Cook for 10 minutes at 356 degrees.

2. Serve while warm.

Note: Freeze any leftover and reheat before serving.

Side Dishes

Fried Avocado Tacos

Nutritional Facts/Calories: 179 calories, 6.07g fat, 26.29g carbohydrates, 4.94g protein

Preparation + Cook Time: 20 minutes

Servings: 12

Ingredients:

Tortillas and toppings 1 egg

1 avocado (divide and remove the seed) 1/2 cup panko breadcrumbs

Salt to taste

Directions/Instructions:

1. Scoop out the meat from each avocado shell and slice them into wedges.

2. Beat the egg in a shallow bowl and put the breadcrumbs in another bowl.

3. Dip the avocado wedges in the beaten egg and coat with the breadcrumbs. Sprinkle them with a bit of salt. Arrange them in the cooking basket in a single layer.

4. Cook for 15 minutes at 392 degrees. Shake the basket halfway through the cooking process.

5. Put the cooked avocado wedges in tortillas and add your preferred toppings.

Roasted Heirloom Tomato with Baked Feta

Nutritional Facts/Calories: 493 calories, 46.23g fat, 8.61g carbohydrates, 12.69g protein

Preparation + Cook Time: 34 minutes

Servings: 4

Ingredients:

1/2 cup red onions (thinly sliced) 1 8-ounce block of feta cheese 2 heirloom tomatoes

1 tablespoon olive oil

A pinch of salt For the basil pesto

1/2 cup olive oil 1 garlic clove

3 tablespoons toasted pine nuts 1/2 cup basil (chopped)

1/2 cup parsley (chopped)

1/2 cup grated parmesan cheese A pinch of salt

Directions/Instructions:

1. Prepare the pesto. Put the toasted pine nuts, garlic, salt, basil, and parmesan in a food processor. Process until combined. Gradually add oil as you mix. Process until everything is blended. Transfer to a bowl and cover. Refrigerate until ready to use.

2. Slice the feta and tomato into round slices with half an inch thickness. Use paper towels to pat them dry.

3. Spread a tablespoon of pesto on top of each tomato slice. Top with a slice of feta.

4. In a small bowl, mix a tablespoon of olive oil and the red onions. Scoop the mixture on top of the feta layer. Arrange them in the cooking basket. Cook for 14 minutes at 390 degrees.

5. Transfer to a platter and add a tablespoon of basil pesto on top of each. Sprinkle them with a bit of salt before serving.

Cheese Sticks

Nutritional Facts/Calories: 255 calories, 13.84g fat, 12.24g carbohydrates, 19.5g protein

Preparation + Cook Time: 30 minutes

Servings: 6

Ingredients:

Marinara sauce for dipping 2 eggs (beaten)

1/4 cup grated Parmesan cheese 1/4 cup all-purpose flour

12 strings of part-skim mozzarella string cheese 2 cups breadcrumbs (Italian seasoned)

Directions/Instructions:

1. Separate the cheese strings and freeze for a couple of hours.

2. Mix to combine the Parmesan cheese and breadcrumbs in a shallow dish.

3. Beat the eggs in a bowl and transfer to a Ziploc bag. Add flour and the frozen cheese strings. Shake until coated.

4.   Dip each string in the beaten egg and coat with the cheese and breadcrumbs mixture.

5.   Arrange 6 pieces cheese string at a time in the cooking basket. Cook for 7 minutes at 400 degrees. Flip the cheese sticks and cook for 3 more minutes. Transfer to a platter and cook the rest of the cheese sticks.

6.   Serve the cooked cheese sticks along with the dipping sauce.

Sweet Potato Fries

Nutritional Facts/Calories: 176 calories, 3.46g fat, 32.78g carbohydrates, 4.08g protein

Preparation + Cook Time: 45 minutes

Servings: 2

Ingredients:

1 sweet potato (rinsed and peeled) 1 tablespoon extra-virgin olive oil 1/2 teaspoon Cajun seasoning

1/2 teaspoon kosher salt

1 teaspoon Parmesan cheese (grated)

Directions/Instructions:

1. Slice the sweet potato into 1/4-inch thick sticks. Put them in a bowl. Add the remaining ingredients and toss until coated.

2. Arrange half of the fries in the cooking basket. Cook for 10 minutes at 400 degrees. Toss the fries halfway through the

cooking process. Transfer the cooked fries to a platter and cook the remaining fries.

2. Season with salt and serve with your preferred dipping sauce.

Air Fried Potato Skins

Nutritional Facts/Calories: 483 calories, 8.73g fat, 92.8g carbohydrates, 12.52g protein

Preparation + Cook Time: 55 minutes

Servings: 2

Ingredients:

1/2 teaspoon olive oil 1/3 cup of sour cream 2 Yukon Gold potatoes 4 bacon strips

1/4 teaspoon of sea salt 2 green onions (minced)

1/4 cup of shredded cheddar cheese

Directions/Instructions:

1. Rinse and scrub the potatoes until clean. Rub with oil and sprinkle with salt. Put them in the cooking basket. Cook for 35 minutes at 400 degrees. Transfer the cooked potatoes to a platter.

2. Put the bacon strip in the cooking basket. Cook for 5 minutes at 400 degrees. Transfer to a plate and leave to cool. Crumble into bits.

3. Slice the potatoes in half. Scoop out most of the meat. Arrange the potato skins with the skin facing side up in the cooking basket. Spray them with oil. Cook for 3 minutes at 400 degrees. Flip the potato skins. Fill each piece with cheese and crumbled bacon. Continue cooking for 2 more minutes.

4. Transfer to a platter. Add a bit of sour cream on top. Sprinkle with minced onion and serve while warm.

Tuscan Style Potato Wedges

Nutritional Facts/Calories: 110 calories, 11.71g fat, 1.12g carbohydrates, 0.3g protein

Preparation + Cook Time: 50 minutes

Servings: 4

Ingredients:

4 Yukon Gold potatoes (cut into wedges) 3 garlic cloves

1/4 teaspoon cayenne pepper 1/2 cup extra-virgin olive oil

1 teaspoon lemon juice 1 teaspoon sea salt

1 sprig of rosemary (remove the leaves and chop)

Directions/Instructions:

1. Mix to combine all ingredients in a bowl. Leave to marinate for 20 minutes. Toss the mixture several times during the process.

2. Arrange half of the potato wedges in the cooking basket. Cook for 9 minutes at 400 degrees. Toss the potato wedges and cook for 3 more minutes. Cook the remaining potato wedges.

3. Serve along with your favorite dipping sauce.

Crispy Brussels Sprouts

Nutritional Facts/Calories: 104 calories, 7.05g fat, 9.31g carbohydrates, 3.38g protein

Preparation + Cook Time: 17 minutes

Servings: 2

Ingredients:

1/2 teaspoon garlic powder 1/4 teaspoon black pepper 1/2 teaspoon salt

1 tablespoon olive oil 10 Brussels sprouts

Directions/Instructions:

1. Rinse Brussel sprouts and pat them dry. Chop off the bottom stem and slice each piece into 2. Put them in a bowl. Add garlic powder, pepper, salt, and olive oil. Toss until coated.

2. Arrange the coated Brussel sprouts in the cooking basket. Cook for 12 minutes at 360 degrees. Shake the basket halfway through the cooking process. Transfer to a plate.

3. Drizzle the cooked Brussel sprouts with a bit of lime juice. Serve along with garlic thyme mayonnaise for dipping.

Appetizer

Grilled Cheese

Nutritional Facts/Calories: 365 calories, 33g fat, 9.5g carbohydrates, 8.7g protein

Preparation + Cook Time: 27 minutes

Servings: 2

Ingredients:

1/4 cup melted butter

1/2 cup sharp cheddar cheese

4 slices of white bread or brioche

Directions/Instructions:

1. Put the cheese in a bowl and the butter in another bowl. Brush all sides of the bread slices with butter. Put cheese on top of 2 bread slices and cover each with the rest of the bread slices.

2. Arrange them in the cooking basket. Cook for 7 minutes at 360 degrees.

Fried Mac and Cheese Balls

Nutritional Facts/Calories: 907 calories, 40.23g fat, 85.74g carbohydrates, 49.99g protein

Preparation + Cook Time: 45 minutes

Servings: 6

Ingredients:

2 cups cream (heated), plus 2 tablespoons for the egg wash Salt and pepper to taste

2 tablespoons all-purpose flour 2 tablespoons unsalted butter 2 eggs

1 pound cheddar cheese (grated) 1 pound elbow macaroni

3 cups seasoned panko breadcrumbs 1/2 pound Parmesan cheese (shredded) 1/2 pound mozzarella cheese (shredded)

Directions/Instructions:

1. Cook the macaroni according to the package directions. Rinse with cold water and drain. Transfer to a bowl and set aside.

2. Melt butter in a saucepan over medium flame. Add flour and whisk for a couple of minutes. Stir the heated cream until there are no

more lumps. Cook until thick. Remove from the stove. Stir in the cheeses until melted. Season with salt and pepper.

3. Pour the cheese mixture over the cooked macaroni. Gently fold until combined. Transfer to a shallow pan and refrigerate for 2 hours.

4. Use your hands to form meatball-sized balls from the mixture. Arrange them in a tray lined with wax paper. Freeze overnight.

5. Prepare the egg wash by combining 2 tablespoons of cream and eggs in a shallow bowl.

6. Dip the frozen mac and cheese balls in the egg wash and coat them with panko breadcrumbs. Gently press to make the coating stick. Arrange them in the cooking basket. Cook for 8 minutes at 400 degrees.

Easy Baked Mac and Cheese

Nutritional Facts/Calories: 470 calories, 16.71g fat, 44.37g carbohydrates, 34.13g protein

Preparation + Cook Time: 19 minutes

Servings: 3

Ingredients:

1/2 cup mozzarella cheese (shredded) 1/4 cup Parmesan cheese (shredded)

3/4 cup cheddar cheese (shredded) 1 cup chicken broth

1 1/2 cups elbow macaroni Salt and pepper to taste 1/2 cup heavy cream

Directions/Instructions:

1. Put the macaroni in a pot with salted water. Lightly boil until half-cooked. This will take about 5 minutes. Drain the liquid and transfer to a bowl.

2. Add the remaining ingredients in the bowl with the cooked macaroni. Season with salt and pepper. Mix until combined. Transfer to a greased baking dish. Place the baking dish in the cooking basket. Cook for 30 minutes at 350 degrees.

Crispy Potato Skin Wedges

Nutritional Facts/Calories: 335 calories, 5.05g fat, 67.15g carbohydrates, 8.01g protein

Preparation + Cook Time: 56 minutes

Servings: 6

Ingredients:

2 tablespoons canola oil 1 1/2 teaspoons paprika 6 russet potatoes

1/2 teaspoon salt

1/2 teaspoon black pepper

Directions/Instructions:

1. Rinse the potatoes and scrub until clean. Put them in a pot with salted water. Boil for 40 minutes until tender. Leave to cool and refrigerate for 30 minutes.

2. In a bowl, mix salt, black pepper, paprika, and canola oil.

3. Slice the potatoes into quarters and put them in a bowl. Add the mixture of oil and spices. Toss until combined.

4. Arrange the potato wedges with the skin side facing down in the cooking basket. Cook for 16 minutes at 390 degrees.

Potato Croquettes

Nutritional Facts/Calories: 704 calories, 25.26g fat, 96.52g carbohydrates, 24.57g protein

Preparation + Cook Time: 38 minutes

Servings: 4

Ingredients:

For the breading

2   eggs (beaten)

3/4 cup breadcrumbs 3/4 cup all-purpose flour

3   tablespoons vegetable oil For the filling

2 egg yolks

4 russet potatoes (peeled and cut into cubes) Salt and pepper to taste

Nutmeg to taste

1   cup grated Parmesan cheese 3 tablespoons chopped chives 2 tablespoons all-purpose flour

Directions/Instructions:

1. Put the cubed potatoes in a pot with salted water. Boil for 15 minutes. Drain the liquid. Transfer the potatoes to a bowl and mash. Leave to cool.

2. In another bowl, combine chives, cheese, flour, and egg yolks. Season with nutmeg, salt, and pepper. Add the mashed potato and mix until combined. Use your hands to form golf-size potato balls. Set them aside.

3. In a shallow bowl, combine the breadcrumbs and oil until loose.

4. Coat each potato ball with flour, dip in the beaten eggs and the oil and breadcrumbs mixture. Shape each coated ball into a cylinder.

5. Arrange the coated potato croquettes in the cooking basket. Cook for 8 minutes at 390 degrees.

Crunchy Eggplant Fries

Nutritional Facts/Calories: 336 calories, 14.95g fat, 35.12g carbohydrates, 17.33g protein

Preparation + Cook Time: 20 minutes

Servings: 2

Ingredients:

2 tablespoons of milk Marinara for dipping

1 eggplant (peeled, cut lengthwise into slices and into 1/4-inch strips)

2 cups seasoned panko breadcrumbs 1 egg (beaten)

1/2 cup Italian cheese blend (shredded)

Directions/Instructions:

1. Whisk the egg and milk in a baking dish until combined.

2. Put cheese and panko breadcrumbs in another baking dish. Mix well.

3. Dip the eggplant slices in the egg mixture and coat them with the breadcrumb mixture.

4. Arrange an even layer of the coated eggplant slices in the cooking basket. Lightly spray them with oil. Cook for 5 minutes at 400 degrees. Transfer to a platter and cook the remaining eggplant slices.

5. Serve while warm along with the marinara sauce for dipping.

Smoked Paprika and Parmesan Potato Wedges

Nutritional Facts/Calories: 199 calories, 5.32g fat, 33.26g carbohydrates, 5.55g protein

Preparation + Cook Time: 35 minutes

Servings: 4

Ingredients:

1/2 teaspoon smoked paprika

1/4 cup Parmesan cheese (grated) 1 tablespoon olive oil

2 Yukon gold potatoes (wash and slice each potato in 6 wedges)

1/4 teaspoon salt

Directions/Instructions:

1. Put the potato wedges in a bowl. Add oil, paprika, and salt. Toss until the wedges are coated. Arrange them in the cooking basket. Cook for 20 minutes at 392 degrees. Shake the basket halfway through the cooking process. Sprinkle Parmesan cheese on top of the potato wedges. Cook for 5 more minutes.

2. Serve while warm.

Zucchini Wedges

Nutritional Facts/Calories: 48 calories, 1.96g fat, 3.45g carbohydrates, 4.14g protein

Preparation + Cook Time: 40 minutes

Servings: 4

Ingredients:

2 medium-sized zucchini

2 egg whites

1/4 teaspoon cayenne pepper 1/4 teaspoon basil

1/4 cup grated Parmesan cheese 1/2 cup panko breadcrumbs

1/4 teaspoon oregano

Directions/Instructions:

1. Mix to combine the herbs, cheese, and crumbs in a bowl. Set aside.

2. Rinse the zucchinis. Slice each piece into 2 in a crosswise manner. Cut each half into wedges.

3. Beat the egg whites in a bowl. Put a bit of the crumb mixture in a shallow bowl.

4. Soak each zucchini wedge in the egg white and coat with the crumb mixture. Add more crumbs if necessary to coat all sides. Refill the bowl with the crumb mixture as you repeat this step to the remaining zucchini wedges.

5. Arrange half of the coated zucchini wedges in a greased cooking basket. Lightly spray them with oil. Cook for 7 minutes at 390 degrees. Flip them and cook for 7 more minutes. Transfer to a platter and loosely cover with foil. Cook the remaining zucchini wedges.

Note: You can serve this along with your favorite dipping sauce, such as ranch or blue cheese dressing.

Snacks

Barbeque Corn Sandwich

Nutritional Facts/Calories: 142 calories, 7.8g fat, 17.9g carbohydrates, 2.4g protein

Preparation + Cook Time: 45 minutes

Servings: 4

Ingredients:

1 capsicum

1 cup sweet corn kernels

2 tablespoon butter (room temperature)

4 slices of white bread (cut the edges and slice the bread horizontally)

For the sauce

1/3 cup stock or water

1/4 teaspoon mustard powder Salt and black pepper to taste

1 1/2 tablespoons tomato ketchup 1/4 cup onion (chopped)

1 teaspoon olive oil

1 garlic flake (crushed) 1/2 tablespoon sugar

1/2 tablespoon Worcestershire sauce 1/2 tablespoon red chili sauce

Directions/Instructions:

1.   Heat oil in a pan over medium-high flame. Add garlic and onions and cook for 4 minutes while stirring often. Add the sugar, chili sauce, mustard, stock, Worcestershire sauce, and tomato ketchup. Mix well and bring to a boil. Turn the heat to low and simmer for 10 minutes. Season with salt and black pepper. Set aside.

2.   Place another pan over medium flame. Melt butter and roast the corn kernels.

3.   Lightly rub a bit of oil on the capsicum. Roast and turn them over until black patches develop. Remove the skin and seeds. Chop it finely and transfer to a bowl. Add the barbecue sauce and roasted corn kernels. Mix well. Spread the mixture on a slice of bread and put another slice on top.

4.   Put the sandwich in the cooking basket. Cook for 15 minutes at

356 degrees. Flip the sandwich halfway through the cooking process.

5.   Serve along with chutney while hot.

Grilled Scallion Cheese Sandwich

Nutritional Facts/Calories: 511 calories, 39.4g fat, 12.9g carbohydrates, 27.6g protein

Preparation + Cook Time: 20 minutes

Servings: 1

Ingredients:

2 teaspoons butter (room temperature) 3/4 cup grated cheddar cheese

2 slices of bread

1 tablespoon grated parmesan cheese 2 scallions (thinly sliced)

Directions/Instructions:

1. Spread a teaspoon of butter on a slice of bread. Place it in the cooking basket with the buttered side facing down. Add scallions and cheddar cheese on top. Spread the rest of the butter in the other slice of bread. Place it on top of the sandwich and sprinkle with Parmesan cheese.

2. Cook for 10 minutes at 356 degrees.

Corn Bread

Nutritional Facts/Calories: 372 calories, 20.16g fat, 39.04g carbohydrates, 8.87g protein

Preparation + Cook Time: 30 minutes

Servings: 4

Ingredients:

1/2 cup whole milk

1/2 cup all-purpose flour 1/2 teaspoon kosher salt 1/4 cup vegetable oil

1/2 cup corn kernels (fresh or frozen) 1/2 cup yellow cornmeal

2 tablespoons sugar

2 eggs

1 1/2 teaspoons baking powder

Directions/Instructions:

1. Combine all the dry ingredients in a bowl and whisk.

2. In another bowl, put all the wet ingredient. Gently mix until combined. Gradually add the dry mixture into the bowl. Mix until smooth. Add the corn and mix until combined.

3. Transfer the mixture into a greased baking dish. Put it in the cooking basket. Cook for 25 minutes at 350 degrees.

4. Allow to cool before transferring to a plate. Slice and serve.

French Fries

Nutritional Facts/Calories: 497 calories, 7.19g fat, 100g carbohydrates, 11.84g protein

Preparation + Cook Time: 1 hour 10 minutes

Servings: 4

Ingredients:

6 russet potatoes (peeled) 2 tablespoons olive oil

Directions/Instructions:

1. Slice the peeled potatoes into strips. Soak them in water for half an hour. Drain and pat excess moisture with paper towels. Put them in a bowl and add oil. Toss until coated.

2. Put the potato slices in the cooking basket. Cook for 30 minutes at 360 degrees. Shake twice during the cooking process.

Snack Mix

Nutritional Facts/Calories: 518 calories, 27g fat, 50.97g carbohydrates, 22.7g protein

Preparation + Cook Time: 25 minutes

Servings: 6

Ingredients:

2 tablespoons melted butter

1 tablespoon Worcestershire sauce 6 cups mixed cereal

1 cup peanuts

1 cup small cheese crackers A pinch of salt

Directions/Instructions:

1. Put the Worcestershire sauce, melted butter, and salt in a bowl. Mix well. Add the nuts, crackers, and cereals, and stir. Transfer the mixture to the cooking basket. Cook for 15 minutes at 320 degrees. Stir the mix every 5 minutes.

2. Transfer to a bowl and leave to cool. Store in an airtight container.

Potatoes Au Gratin

Nutritional Facts/Calories: 429 calories, 7.27g fat, 81.05g carbohydrates, 12.82g protein

Preparation + Cook Time: 35 minutes

Servings: 6

Ingredients:

1/2 cup grated semi-mature cheese 1/2 cup milk

1/2 cup cream

7 russet potatoes (peeled) 1/2 teaspoon of nutmeg

1 teaspoon of black pepper

Directions/Instructions:

1. Slice the peeled potatoes thinly.

2. Combine the cream and milk in a bowl. Season with nutmeg, salt, and pepper. Add the potato slices and toss until coated.

3. Arrange the coated potato slices in a baking dish. Pour the seasoning mixture on top. Put the baking dish inside the cooking basket. Cook for 25 minutes at 390 degrees.

Rosemary Russet Potato Chips

Nutritional Facts/Calories: 322 calories, 3.69g fat, 66g carbohydrates, 7.5g protein

Preparation + Cook Time: 1 hour 10 minutes

Servings: 4

Ingredients:

2 teaspoons rosemary (chopped) 1 tablespoon olive oil

4 russet potatoes 1/2 teaspoon salt

Directions/Instructions:

1. Rinse the potatoes and scrub to clean. Peel and cut them in a lengthwise manner similar to thin chips. Put them in a bowl and soakin water for 30 minutes. Change the water several times during this period. Drain the liquid. Pat the potato chips with paper towels to dry.

2.   Toss the chips in a bowl with olive oil. Transfer them to the cooking basket. Cook for 30 minutes at 330 degrees. Shake several times during the cooking process.

3.   Toss the cooked chips in a bowl with salt and rosemary while warm.

Crunchy Onion Rings

Nutritional Facts/Calories: 140 calories, 0.45g fat, 30.04g carbohydrates, 3.9g protein

Preparation + Cook Time: 45 minutes

Servings: 4

Ingredients:

1/2 teaspoon garlic powder A bowl of ice water

1 sweet onion (thinly sliced) 1 cup self-rising flour

1 teaspoon paprika

1   teaspoon salt

Directions/Instructions:

1. Put the onion slices in the bowl with ice water and soak for 10 minutes.

2. Put flour in a bowl and mix it with paprika, salt, pepper, and garlic powder.

3. Use a pair of tongs to get the onions from the bowl with water. Drain and put them in the seasoned flour. Toss to coat.

4. Arrange the first batch in the cooking basket. Lightly spray with oil. Cook for 7 minutes at 400 degrees. Shake twice or thrice during the cooking process. Cook the rest of the coated onions.

Yummy Donuts

Nutritional Facts/Calories: 261 calories, 5g fat, 46g carbohydrates, 7.9g protein

Preparation + Cook Time: 45 minutes

Servings: 6

Ingredients:

2 tablespoons condensed milk (add 1 tablespoon of cocoa powder for icing)

2 tablespoons icing sugar (for icing) 2 teaspoons vanilla essence

1 cup whole wheat flour 3/4 cup sugar

1 egg

1/2 teaspoon salt

2 teaspoons baking powder

1 cup all-purpose flour (add more for dusting)

1 tablespoon butter 1/2 cup milk

Directions/Instructions:

1.	In a bowl, sift to combine salt, baking powder, all-purpose flour, and whole wheat flour.

2.	In another bowl, beat the egg and sugar until fluffy. Fold in the sifted dry ingredients. Add butter, vanilla essence, and milk. Mix until combined but do not over knead. Chill for an hour.

3.	Transfer the chilled dough to a floured surface. Roll it into 1/2-inch thickness. Use any round object or a doughnut cutter to shape the dough into donuts. Use a smaller circular object to make smaller holes in the middle of each donut.

4.	Cook in batches. Arrange the first batch in the cooking basket. Cook for 8 minutes at 390 degrees. Transfer to a plate and cook the rest of the donuts.

5.	Leave the donuts to cool. Sprinkle some pieces with icing sugar. Glaze the rest with chocolate syrup.

French Fries with Vegan Mushroom Gravy

Nutritional Facts/Calories: 510 calories, 11g fat, 69g carbohydrates, 16g protein

Preparation + Cook Time: 45 minutes

Servings: 4

Ingredients:

1/4 teaspoon ground black pepper 1/4 teaspoon granulated garlic

1/2 teaspoon salt

1/2 teaspoon smoked paprika

1 teaspoon Cajun seasoning blend 2 teaspoons olive oil

6 cups boiling water

4 medium russet potatoes (slice into 2 and cut into planks) For the gravy

1 tablespoon tapioca starch 1/2 cup water

2 teaspoons vegan Worcestershire sauce 2 teaspoons soy sauce

3 cups mushrooms (chopped) 1 tablespoon olive oil

Directions/Instructions:

1. Put the fries in a saucepan. Add boiling water and leave for 15 minutes to soak. Drain water and pat the fries with paper towels to dry. Put them in a bowl. Add olive oil, black pepper, garlic, salt, paprika, and Cajun seasoning. Toss until coated.

2. Arrange the seasoned fries in the cooking basket. Cook for 5 minutes at 350 degrees. Shake the basket and continue cooking for

5 more minutes. Turn the temperature to 390 degrees and cook for 5 minutes. Shake the basket and continue cooking for 5 more minutes.

3. Prepare the gravy. Put a tablespoon of olive oil in a pan over medium flame. Add the mushrooms and cook until they start releasing juices. Add the Worcestershire sauce and soy sauce. Cook for 2 minutes while you stir. Add tapioca starch and water. Mix well. Cook on a medium-high flame until thick.

4. Serve the fries along with the gravy.

Dessert

Vanilla Soufflé

Nutritional Facts/Calories: 215 calories, 12.2g fat, 18.98g carbohydrates, 6.66g protein

Preparation + Cook Time: 52 minutes

Servings: 6

Ingredients:

1/4 cup softened butter 1/4 cup sugar

1/4 cup all-purpose flour 5 egg whites

4 egg yolks

1 teaspoon cream of tartar 2 teaspoons vanilla extract 1 vanilla bean

1-ounce sugar

1 cup whole milk

Directions/Instructions:

1. Mix the butter and flour in a bowl until the mixture becomes a smooth paste.

2. Heat milk in a pan over medium flame. Add sugar and stir until dissolved. Add the vanilla bean and bring to a boil. Beat the mixture using a wire whisk as you add the butter and flour mixture. Continue whisking until there are no more lumps. Reduce the heat to low and simmer until thick. Discard the vanilla bean. Turn off the heat.

3. Place them on an ice bath and allow to cool for 10 minutes.

4. Grease 6 ramekins with butter. Sprinkle each with a bit of sugar.

5. Beat the egg yolks in a bowl. Add the vanilla extract and milk mixture. Mix until combined.

6. In another bowl, beat the egg whites, cream of tartar and sugar until it forms medium stiff peaks. Gradually fold the egg whites into the soufflé base. Transfer the mixture to the ramekins.

7. Put 3 ramekins in the cooking basket at a time. Cook for 16 minutes at 330 degrees. Transfer to a wire rack to cool and cook the rest.

8. Sprinkle powdered sugar on top and drizzle with chocolate sauce before serving.

Chocolate Marshmallow Bread Pudding

Nutritional Facts/Calories: 741 calories, 48.5g fat, 60.23g carbohydrates, 15.6g protein

Preparation + Cook Time: 55 minutes

Servings: 4

Ingredients:

2   1/2 cups heavy cream

1 teaspoon pure vanilla extract 1 teaspoon fresh lemon juice 1/2 cup mini marshmallows 3/4 cup sugar

1/4 cup chocolate chips 1/2 teaspoon kosher salt 4 eggs

5 croissants (sliced into 1-inch cubes)

Directions/Instructions:

1. Put the eggs, cream, lemon juice, salt, vanilla extract, and sugar in a blender. Process until smooth.

2. Arrange the cubed croissant in the cooking basket. Cook for 5 minutes at 400 degrees.

3. Soak the toasted croissant cubes in the custard mixture. Transfer the mixture to a greased baking dish. Add the marshmallows and chocolate chips. Gently stir.

4. Put the baking dish in the cooking basket. Cook for 25 minutes at 340 degrees.

5. Top with whipped cream and serve while warm.

Chocolate Cake Version 1

Nutritional Facts/Calories: 377 calories, 14.62g fat, 57g carbohydrates, 5.58g protein

Preparation + Cook Time: 35 minutes

Servings: 4

Ingredients:

1 cup water

3/4 cup granulated sugar 1 tablespoon white vinegar 1 teaspoon baking soda

1 teaspoon pure vanilla extract 1/4 cup vegetable oil

1/2 teaspoon kosher salt

3 tablespoons cocoa powder (unsweetened) 1 1/2 cups all-purpose flour

Directions/Instructions:

1. Put all the ingredients in a bowl. Mix using a hand mixer at a low- speed setting until combined. Transfer the batter to a greased baking dish.

2. Put the baking dish in the cooking basket. Cook for 30 minutes at 330 degrees.

3. Top with whipped cream and serve while warm.

Chocolate Cake Version 2

Nutritional Facts/Calories: 333 calories, 14.48g fat, 46.2g carbohydrates, 5.58g protein

Preparation + Cook Time: 50 minutes

Servings: 10

Ingredients:

6 tablespoons cocoa powder 1/2 teaspoon baking soda

1 teaspoon baking powder

9 tablespoons unsalted butter

2/3 cup caster sugar 2 teaspoons vanilla 1/2 cup sour cream 1 cup flour

3 eggs

For the chocolate icing:

5.5 ounces chocolate 1 teaspoon vanilla

1 2/3 cups icing sugar

3 1/2 tablespoons unsalted butter (room temperature)

Directions/Instructions:

1. Put all the ingredients for the cake in a food processor. Process until combined. Transfer to a baking dish.

2. Put the baking dish in the cooking basket. Cook for 35 minutes at 320 degrees. Transfer to a wire rack and leave to cool.

3. Melt the chocolate in the microwave. Let it cool down a bit before adding to the remaining ingredients for the icing.

4. Transfer the cake to a plate. Spread the icing all over. Slice and serve.

Apricot Blackberry Crumble

Nutritional Facts/Calories: 217 calories, 7.44g fat, 36.2g carbohydrates, 2.3g protein

Preparation + Cook Time: 30 minutes

Servings: 8

Ingredients:

5.5 ounces fresh blackberries

18 ounces fresh apricots (remove the seeds and cut into cubes) Salt to taste

2 tablespoons lemon juice 5 tablespoons cold butter 1 cup flour

1/2 cup sugar

Directions/Instructions:

1. Put the apricots and blackberries in a bowl. Add lemon juice and 2 tablespoons of sugar. Mix until combined. Transfer the mixture to a baking dish.

2.   Put flour, the rest of the sugar, and a pinch of salt in a bowl. Mix well. Add a tablespoon of cold butter. Use your hands to combine the mixture until it becomes crumbly. Put this on top of the fruit mixture and press it down lightly.

3.   Place the baking dish in the cooking basket. Cook for 20 minutes at 390 degrees.

4.   Allow to cool before slicing and serving.

Peanut Butter Marshmallow Fluff Turnovers

Nutritional Facts/Calories: 526 calories, 31.75g fat, 55.55g carbohydrates, 6.31g protein

Preparation + Cook Time: 20 minutes

Servings: 4

Ingredients:

4 tablespoons chunky peanut butter A pinch of sea salt

4 sheets filo pastry (thawed) 2 ounces melted butter

4 teaspoons marshmallow fluff

Directions/Instructions:

1. Lay a sheet of filo pastry on a flat surface. Brush it with melted butter. Put another sheet on top and brush it with butter. Repeat the step to the rest of the sheets. Cut the layers of buttered filo sheets into four 12x3-inch strips.

2.   Put a teaspoon of marshmallow fluff and a tablespoon of peanut butter at the bottom of each strip. Fold it repeatedly until you have formed a triangle with the filling carefully wrapped. Seal the ends of the sheets with a touch of butter.

3.   Arrange the finished turnovers in the cooking basket. Cook for 5 minutes at 360 degrees.

White Chocolate Raspberry Cheesecake Rolls

Nutritional Facts/Calories: 123 calories, 2.24g fat, 21.64g carbohydrates, 3.57g protein

Preparation + Cook Time: 28 minutes

Servings: 10

Ingredients:

1/4 cup white chocolate chips Powdered sugar for dusting

2 1/2 cups cheesecake filling 10 egg roll wrappers

1 pint fresh raspberries

Directions/Instructions:

1. Spread an eggroll wrapper on a cutting board. Scoop 1/4 cup of the cheesecake filling at the center of the wrapper. Add 5 raspberries and white chocolate chips. Fold each corner to on top of each other until the filling is completely covered. Damp the tip of the last corner before folding. Roll the piece until tight.

2. Perform the sequence above with the remaining egg roll wrappers.

3. Arrange 5 rolls in the cooker basket of the fryer at a time. Lightly spray them with oil. Cook for 7 minutes at 400 degrees. Flip the rolls and continue cooking for 2 minutes. Transfer to a plate. Cook the remaining rolls.

4. Sprinkle the rolls with powdered sugar and serve while warm.

Fried Dough

Nutritional Facts/Calories: 199 calories, 7.14g fat, 29.54g carbohydrates, 24.26g protein

Preparation + Cook Time: 39 minutes

Servings: 12

Ingredients:

2 teaspoons kosher salt 1 teaspoon honey

Powdered sugar for dusting 3 1/2 to 4 cups bread flour

1 envelope of instant dry yeast

1 1/2 cups warm water (110 degrees) 2 tablespoons grapeseed oil

Directions/Instructions:

1. Put salt, flour, yeast, and honey in a bowl. Use an electric mixer to combine the ingredients. Add grapeseed oil and water as you mix. Mix until a dough forms. Use your hands to shape the dough into a ball. Add water if it is too dry or flour if it is too sticky.

2.   Put the dough on a slightly floured surface. Knead it until smooth and divide into 4. Leave for 20 minutes to rest.

3.   Press each ball firmly until flat. Lightly spray both sides with oil. Put it in the cooking basket. Cook for 3 minutes at 400 degrees. Flip the dough and cook for 3 more minutes. Repeat the step to the rest of the dough.

4.   Arrange the cooked dough on a plate and sprinkle with powdered sugar on top.

Pumpkin Cupcakes

Nutritional Facts/Calories: 243 calories, 11.06g fat, 31g carbohydrates, 5.49g protein

Preparation + Cook Time: 46 minutes

Servings: 12

Ingredients:

2 eggs

1 cup all-purpose flour (sifted) 1/4 teaspoon kosher salt

1 1/2 teaspoons vanilla extract 1/2 teaspoon baking powder 1/2 cup sugar

2 teaspoons pumpkin pie spice

1/2 cup pumpkin puree (canned or fresh) 1 stick of unsalted butter (softened)

For the maple cream frosting (for 24 cupcakes)

2 tablespoons unsalted butter (softened) 2 cups powdered sugar (sifted)

1 8-ounce package cream cheese 2 teaspoons maple extract

Directions/Instructions:

1. Sift the flour together with baking powder, salt, and pie spice. Set aside.

2. Mix butter and sugar in another bowl using a hand mixer for 3 minutes or until fluffy. Add the eggs, pumpkin puree, and vanilla. Mix until creamy. Gradually add the dry ingredients. Mix until well- combined.

3. Fill 2/3 of each muffin cup lined with a cupcake liner with the batter. Arrange 4 muffin cups in the cooking basket at a time. Cook each batch for 12 minutes at 350 degrees.

4. Put the cooked cupcakes to a wire rack to cool. Top with maple cream cheese frosting and sprinkle with brown sugar.

Here are the steps to make the maple cream frosting:

1. Put the cream cheese and butter in a bowl and mix using an electric mixer until smooth. Add the maple extract and gradually add the powdered sugar. Continue mixing until fluffy.

Glazed Air-Fried Donuts

Nutritional Facts/Calories: 481 calories, 3.64g fat, 40.43g carbohydrates, 4.94g protein

Preparation + Cook Time: 55 minutes

Servings: 4

Ingredients:

1 16-ounce can of vanilla frosting

1 8-ounce can of refrigerated croissant dinner rolls (sliced into 1-inch rounds)

Directions/Instructions:

1. Slice a hole in the middle of each rounded croissant. Arrange 5 pieces in the cooking basket at a time. Lightly spray them with oil. Cook for 2 minutes at 400 degrees. Flip the doughnuts and cook for 3 more minutes. Transfer to a plate and cook the remaining doughnuts.

2. Place 1/2 cup of the frosting in a heat-proof bowl. Microwave for 30 seconds. Drizzle on top of the cooked doughnuts. Leave to cool until the frosting is set.

Conclusion

I hope this book was able to help you to understand the benefits of an Air Fryer and the basics on how to use it. The next step is to plan your meals and gather the ingredients.

This appliance is easy to use and you will eventually get the hang of the process. Once you have tried several recipes, you can already start tweaking the ingredients to create variations or start making your own.

Enjoy the process of preparing your meals in a healthier way using this innovation when it comes to cooking.

www.ingramcontent.com/pod-product-compliance
Lightning Source LLC
Chambersburg PA
CBHW071613080526
44588CB00010B/1121